"Orlando brilliantly [illegible]
work while simultaneously inspiring us to find meaning and purpose in our careers. This is a must read for anyone eager to drive personal success."

—**Shari Krull,** *Executive Director, Streetwise Partners*

"As someone who has been in Orlando's orbit for many years and watched him ascend in his career, what he shares in this book is authentic. He knows himself, he sets ambitious goals, he takes calculated risks, he keeps a steady pace, and appreciates the quality of relationships he's built along the way. Great advice from a great leader."

—**Jennifer Longnion**, *Former COO, Dollar Shave Club, Inc. and Founder of See & Free Consulting*

"With How Did You Get That Job?, Orlando Ashford takes you on a journey that includes perspectives and pearls of wisdom that will prove relevant regardless of where you may be on your career journey. His insights are particularly important as a Black man who has navigated numerous levels and layers of corporate life. His sense of humor and down to earth personality complement his results oriented business focus and make for an enjoyable and informative read."

—**Clyde Walker,** *Board Chair, First Choice Health / Retired SVP, Human Resources, Continental Mills*

""How did you get that job?" is a true roadmap to personal and career success. Orlando's practical account provides real and tangible strategies to realizing your maximum career trajectory. No matter the stage of your career, read it, internalize it and live by it. You won't be sorry!"

–Eric Hutcherson, *Chief People & Inclusion Officer at Universal Music Group*

"Orlando has really captured the key concepts for how to successfully navigate the corporate environment. I've know him for a long time and have seen several of these stories unfold firsthand. I'm excited to see him share them with others for their benefit. A must read for a person with ambition."

–Roy Weathers, *Vice Chair, PwC*

"Orlando provides powerful advice and delivers a blueprint to help you create the career you want. "How did you get that job?" challenges you to be intentional about navigating your career journey and making an impact by using your own uniqueness as a strength."

–Billy Dexter, *Managing Director, Heidrick & Struggles.*
Author - Making your Net-Work

How did you get THAT JOB?

8 PRINCIPLES TO ACCELERATE YOUR CAREER AND SOAR IN CORPORATE AMERICA

ORLANDO ASHFORD

How did you get THAT JOB?

Published by Fig Factor Media, LLC
Cover Design & Layout by Juan Pablo Ruiz
Printed in the United States of America

ISBN: 978-1-952779-05-3
Library of Congress Control Number: 2020917665

TABLE OF CONTENTS:

PREFACE

I am not a rocket.

While I have been called that by colleagues as a way to describe what some see as meteoric career success, let me set the record straight right here: I am not a rocket. If you hadn't heard it before, the term is tossed around for people with ambitious corporate assent. It's not unusual for "rockets" to hear a question I've been asked a thousand times after speeches, or in the quiet shush of a plushly-carpeted hallway outside a boardroom, or by friends and former colleagues: "How did you get THAT job?"

Sure, at 27 I was a Director at Ameritech; at 31, I was the youngest partner at Delta Consulting; at 39, I was named chief human resources officer at Marsh & McLennan; at 42, I was named to the Board of Directors at the multi-billion-dollar manufacturer ITT; at 45, I ran a $600 million P&L for Mercer Consulting, and at 46, I was named President of Holland America Line. All of that is true. But all of that does not make a person a rocket.

Rockets do soar into space, but there is no air in space. There are no people, no whiteboards, no after-work drinks at five on a Friday during the summer. Rockets follow Newton's third law: for every action, there's an equal and opposite reaction. If being a rocket is ascending to a lonely place where good intentions are met with bad outcomes, then no thanks.

I believe in people. I believe that positivity, self-worth,

mentorship, and courage open doors. I believe we are all navigating career paths that are a direct extension of our life paths. And it's not easy–particularly in times of disruption and uncertainty which is, when you think about it, always upon us in some way.

I want to help you navigate your path. Using my experience as a guide, I like to think of this book as a guide to accelerate the adventure of life, and your life's work.

And, as an African American who has navigated the corporate landscape of today's world, I have a unique perspective that I think could also be particularly valuable to people of difference–in particular, people of color, young people, and all those who wish to make a difference with the time and effort they invest in their careers.

This book is a conversation between you and me. I will show you the principles I've lived by, learned by, failed by, and succeeded by–so you walk away with greater clarity, guidance, and tools to achieve professional success, however you define it. Whether that means a path to the C-suite, senior management, entrepreneurship, or something else, the choice is yours.

–Orlando Ashford

September 2020

INTRODUCTION

This book is intended to serve as a collection of "rules and tools" to help you navigate the intricate social dynamics of the workplace. Managing positive relationships with people like your boss, your peers, your subordinates, and all those along your career path leads to visible impact and accelerates your career success.

We will review some of the major lessons I've learned through experiences in my nearly 30 years working in corporate America, including roles with major Fortune 500 companies, like Andersen Consulting (now Accenture), Ameritech, Delta Consulting, Motorola, Coca-Cola, Marsh & McLennan, and Carnival Corporation.

Everything starts with having a vision for yourself--a picture of what you want from your career. Whenever I begin a coaching session, my first question is, what do you want to be when you grow up? What do you want from your career? We are going to work through this question for you, because a successful career starts with a vision. I will challenge you to paint this picture for yourself, and then we will dive into the key considerations for you to maximize your career journey.

We will also review a simple but critical concept to career success: Delivering results. If you can't draw a clear line between the work you do and its impact on the business, you are in the wrong role to achieve promotion and success. The rest doesn't matter if you don't get things done and deliver results. Once we've built your career vision and determined you are a "work killer," then we will explore important concepts to consider in enabling your effectiveness at work and your ascension up the corporate ladder.

Taking calculated risks will be an important part of your career journey. We'll discuss how to think about risk and what risks will be most helpful in determining career progression. Are you a "culture carrier" in your organization? Do you build and promote the desired organizational culture, or do you pull the culture down? A culture is the summation of beliefs, behaviors, and assumptions. It's important to be a "culture builder" in an organization, and we'll explore how to do that. Those who build the culture of an organization often get to lead more of that organization.

An important concept I want to ground you in is the idea of "chess boards." Each role, job, or area of interest to you is a chess board. I'll encourage you to give yourself flexibility by playing several at the same time. I'll refer to this concept throughout the book. Having multiple boards in play at the same time gives you power.

And we will work on building your personal brand. When your name comes up for promotion or job consideration, what do people say? What's your reputation? You can influence what people say by investing in your personal brand. I'll share some thoughts on how to do that.

The concept of networking is often touted as an important aspect of being successful, but this concept is often misunderstood. We'll move beyond simply collecting business cards at business mixers into building a "career community." A team of resources you can tap into for ideas, advice, and counsel becomes increasingly important over the course of your career. I will explore this concept with you and show you ways to build your community.

I also think it's important to explore the power of being different in the workplace. In today's environment of passionate debate and discussion about diversity, inclusion, and social justice, I believe it's important for all of us to leverage and celebrate our own unique genius. Our differences make us more valuable, insightful, and powerful in our contributions if you know how to harness that uniqueness.

I will share some of my perspectives on how to leverage being different, coming from the perspective of an African American executive and some of the personal experiences that I've had to navigate. I'll share my perspectives and how I've managed my feelings and reactions over the years as examples of how to manage reactions to your differences–yours and others'.

How do you respond when you are "the only one in the room?" Is it a source of insecurity or power? Because, while unfortunate and not right, this can be an opportunity to change the framing and lean into your uniqueness. I'm excited to share why I believe there is power in being different. I think it's important not only for work, but for life.

Let's begin.

"You become what you believe."
—Oprah Winfrey

CHAPTER 1

Envision Your Future

I've always thought about my work, and each role I've had, as part of a career. And what's a career? A career is a mixture of experiences—education, events, networks, and relationships--that can come together in an infinite number of ways.

Certainly, if you start with a solid foundation you have the strong possibility of a successful career. Even so, it is important to pay attention to some key details along the way. Building a successful career for yourself is a process that rewards a bit of vision, experimentation, individualization, and, ultimately, freedom.

I learned this with my own career path, and I would like to share with you the wide range of elements that I believe go into the making of a solid career. I will also share the key concepts that are critical to pulling these elements together so you might integrate them in a way that allows you to extract the maximum amount of value.

You own your education and experience, and those come together to have some value in the job market. You trade that value for roles or jobs, and over time, you build a career. It sounds simple, but we both know there is much more to it. We will explore the nuances to consider as you move through your career journey.

My dad used to tell me, "The only thing you have is your name. You want to make sure that you deliver value and don't do things that take away from that." My dad was right. A good education, a variety of strategic experiences, and a good reputation make a difference and have helped bolster my trajectory.

The workplace has evolved

Let's put the first principle of envisioning your future into play by looking at the new world of work.

Oftentimes, when people think of innovation, they think of something that is revealed suddenly, like a Big Bang. Most innovations, however, are not a Big Bang, but are instead a collection of small, executable steps that allow you to learn something, then try something else. We're moving toward a work world that is much more open and flexible, where one can plug in, then unplug, and plug in somewhere else. This system allows for more creativity, innovation, and collaboration than in prior generations.

The days of joining a company and having a basic roadmap to follow for the next thirty years, then retiring with a gold watch are basically gone. In our new corporate reality, things will be much more varied, and therefore, less predictable. Those who like the concept of creativity, innovation, collaboration and surprise, will thrive in this new world. Those who want everything mapped out, and want promises made up front, will struggle because "we'll build as we go" is the world of the future.

I think many of our young people are more comfortable with a less predictable lifestyle, but they've also adjusted their expectations to match. In an effort to create more of that flexibility, many young people today are putting off buying their first home an average of seven of years later than previous generations, and are staying in their parents' home longer. They may think, "Why do I need to rush out into the world and take on a lot of debt just to trap myself into the situation my parents were trapped in? I want to maintain flexibility. I will stay home longer, and put off buying that first house longer. I will maintain more flexibility financially, which allows me to maintain more flexibility in my lifestyle. I am going to travel vs. having a mortgage or car payment. I want to live some now vs. waiting until I retire. And, because I'll have more flexibility, I can build a career that meets my interests and excites me."

Anyone looking into the future of the nature of work knew that working from home would increase, but the COVID-19 pandemic that began at the end of 2019 has fundamentally and permanently accelerated that change. Polls taken of major employers are already reflecting that the percentage of workers who will go back to work in the office at even 50 percent is way down from where it was pre-pandemic, and many employers report that more than half of their work force will remain working from home after the pandemic has passed. Working from home has finally become the new normal.

A good friend and chief human resources officer of a major health care company, Doug Parks, recently wrote about the "Future of Work,"

"The 'future of work' includes the reskilling, upskilling, and redeployment of the workforce as job requirements change. We know those who have been hardest hit by job losses in this pandemic have been people of color, women, and workers with lower incomes. HR has the opportunity–I would argue it is our obligation to lead as community citizens–to craft a plan to help those who have lost work start thinking about the alternatives that could be available to them instead of waiting for things to return back to the way they were. Remote work inherently means workers will need digital skills in roles for which it wasn't a necessity before. Employer-led partnerships that aim to invest in developing broad-based programs and a digital foundation to help upskill employees builds resiliency in our organizations and communities as workers become competitive for jobs that can be performed anywhere, now and in the future."

What was thought to be a future need for businesses to reassess the way they do business is happening now.

Nonetheless, more than 60 percent of today's workers continue to be disengaged in their jobs. They don't like what they do for work, but they do it because they need the income to provide for their family, or meet whatever financial commitments they've made.

Those of us from older generations sometimes criticize young people for not trying hard enough in the way we think they should be trying. But, the truth is, many of us are actually quietly jealous of them and their freedom.

A very good friend of mine is super smart and talented, but feels trapped in his job. He says, "I need this paycheck. I've got kids in school." I encourage him to start his own business, but he says he can't. He's so deep in the current game that it would be difficult to extract himself from the system and start over. It doesn't matter that he has skills and talents that would allow him to be quite successful. He just doesn't have the flexibility.

I don't have a simple answer for how more established professionals can move forward with this new way of thinking. Young people have the option of starting out building their lives in a more flexible way, but those of us who are in the middle of our careers need to figure out how to maximize our current value, planning for our second or third careers. It may not be a simple answer, but you can teach an old dog new tricks. We'll discuss this more later.

In this game called Corporate America, there are nuances for people of color, and other people of difference, and how we show up: additional obstacles, issues to manage, things to overcome. Simply navigating the corporate maze.

Yet, even as I give advice targeted to these specific groups, I believe this guidance also applies to a general audience in pursuit of a long-term corporate career, to all of those with ambition and aspiration.

What makes a job a career

What skills do you have? What can you do so well that people are willing to hire you, trade with you, or seek you out for help? What's that collection of skills and capabilities that are uniquely yours that you can trade against? These are the tools that will make your career successful.

And, there is a difference between a job and a career. With a job, the organization owns the means of production, and you have been asked to execute a set of duties for which you will be paid. At any time, you or the company could decide to make a change, and somebody else can take your place.

A career really centers on a mindset, a knowledge base, and a set of experiences that have value, which you own, and can execute and deliver. The ability to carry that with you allows you to build a career. You can deliver and execute it in multiple places, locations, scenes, and settings.

Envisioning

I do a lot of public speaking, and I especially enjoy talking to students in high school and college about building their future careers. Often, the students I speak to are from disadvantaged backgrounds and grew up without privilege. So, when I speak with them, I ask them to envision who they can become--someone who looks like them, who wears a nice suit, drives a nice car, makes it through college and into corporations, not just in the entertainment business or in sports, which is so often the path they believe is their best chance at success.

I coach as many young people one-on-one as possible, and when we meet, I'm usually asked for help with their career choices and to give them feedback based on my own experiences.

Ralph Waldo Emerson said,

> "The mind, once stretched by a new idea, never returns to its original dimensions."

This is an idea that has always stuck with me, and my hope is that learning through my experiences will help stretch your mind to advance your career. You can't stretch it by yourself. You have to collaborate with other people, using other tools, and creating new opportunities in order to create change.

You may currently have things in your career that are working but, like most of us, also have things that aren't working well. Looking to books you read, people you talk to, quotes that stick with you, things you see in the media, things you learn, and things you disagree with, I encourage you to think about what is possible. This is how you create your vision for what you want to be, and that vision will continue to evolve, because your brain will continue to stretch with time and knowledge. It's like a perpetual process of improvement, with more and better elements as you go.

And if there is one thing you can do that will help your career be all you hope it will be, it is to *envision* it. So, think BIG.

Envision your career and your life

"What do you want to be when you grow up?" Most of us were asked that as a child, or even as a teenager or young adult. Now people ask, "Have you considered your career path?" No matter how people ask it, the question is still the same. "What kind of work do you want to do when you enter the workforce?"

Ask yourself the same question, "What do I want to do when I enter the workforce?" It's the best question to ask at any age because it focuses on the career and life you want for yourself, not on what other people want for you. Too many people go through life taking what it throws at them. They don't realize they have a choice about where they go, what they do, and who they become. Instead of shaping and defining their lives, they let life define and shape them. Life, and the opportunities, gifts, and skills we have do influence us, but they don't have to control us.

Our parents, friends, family, and circumstances can also pressure us to follow a path we don't want to follow. Sometimes choosing a career is the easy part and pursuing it against all opposition and circumstances is the challenge.

Get outside your head

Studies have shown that people who write down their goals and review them daily are 42 percent more likely to actually accomplish those goals. It's the same with envisioning a career. You've got to write down your vision. However, writing down the vision is only one ingredient in your success plan. You've got to also write down the tactics that will actually help you reach that vision. There are a lot of people who say that they want to be rich and famous. I say, "That's great. What does that mean? So, what's rich? What does that mean? Famous, how do you define that?"

What's the first executable step that you need to take in order to create it? How much money makes you rich? To a kid $20, or $50, or $100 is rich. To someone working at a fast food restaurant for $12 an hour, a job that pays $50 or $100 an hour may feel rich. So, I ask, what is rich to you? You'll realize that the more money you make, the more that concept of "rich" will change. When you've made six figures a year, you'll want to make seven figures, then eight, and so on. Our perceptions change when our reality changes. You need to envision your career in detail, so you'll know when you've reached your goals.

I have a friend who works at a bar and loves the business,

the people, and the atmosphere--everything about it. Bars are his passion. He talks about how he wants to own his own bar, but he doesn't take the steps to actually do it. I'm not sure if he just expects someone to walk in and say, "Wow, you make a mean Manhattan, here's a bar," or what. But until he takes some action, nothing is going to happen.

The first step is visualizing what your life would be like if you had your dream career, and then you have to take steps to getting there.

Once you have your vision statement – I want to open up a bar; I want to be SVP of Marketing; I want to be CEO of a large non-profit; I want to run a tech start-up – then ask yourself, "What are the things I need to do in order to be able to do that?"

You may not know the answers yet, so ask questions. Ask people who already own a bar what they had to do. Find the licensing organization for bars and ask them. Check out schools and conferences and courses on owning a bar. Look at the skill set and experiences you'll need – accounting, business, marketing, etc. As you ask those questions, you'll get different perspectives. Some will be clear to you and will resonate; some will be contradictory. That's where you have to internalize what you have heard and make some personal decisions. Eventually, you have to move from data collection to action. You have to take that first actionable step, and then the next one, and from there, you keep moving forward, holding yourself accountable to take the necessary steps to reach your end goal.

Do what makes you come alive

I might have been thrilled to discover my calling, but my parents weren't nearly as excited as I was. They wanted me to be an engineer. It was safe and transferrable. I would make a good living, and be set for my life journey ahead. My parents only wanted to set me up for success, and they had a fairly specific idea of how that was most likely to happen.

So, in hindsight maybe I could have leveraged my developing diplomacy skills a bit better than I did. Instead, I came home freshman year and without much preamble I said, "Hey Dad, I want to change my major."

Now, growing up, the thought in my family was that I could be a doctor, a lawyer, or an engineer. At the time I was studying engineering, so when I told my father I wanted to change my major, he said, "To what, doctor or lawyer?" In my father's mind, those were the only other two choices I had. I said, "No, I want to change my major to organizational leadership."

I started describing this area of study and he cut me a look like, "That doesn't sound like anything you can make any money doing. And, as long as I'm helping you…" He was pretty clear about what he would or wouldn't support. I was on partial scholarship, I was paying for part of my education, and my parents were paying the rest. They weren't very supportive of me changing my major to organizational leadership, and since they were helping fund my degree, they insisted that I stay in engineering. They had a say in what I did because they had a financial investment in me.

My junior year, I got a job as a resident assistant (RA). At Purdue, as an RA, you got room, board, and the cost of your tuition covered by the job. So, essentially, I was paying my own way and midway through my junior year I changed my major. I was three-and-a-half years into my industrial engineering degree when I got my RA job, but I changed my major the next day.

You may or may not have to deal with opposition from family, parents, friends, or co-workers—even yourself—but chances are someone in your life is not going to be supportive of your choice. Learn to recognize what you want and commit to it. I'm not saying my parents were wrong. I think it's our parents' job to take the knowledge, information, and perspective they have to encourage you and provide direction. But you have to assess the worst-case scenario and make a decision for yourself.

I was still in a good school and was still going to graduate. People in organizational leadership were still getting good jobs, although definitely paying less, but it was a scenario I could live with. The advice my parents were giving me wasn't bad advice. Being a doctor, a lawyer, or an engineer are all wonderful careers, and those who do those things generally do well. But I also believe you have to figure out what the thing is that you're most passionate about. If you do something you're really passionate about, the money will come, if money is part of your ambition.

It's not that I didn't like or want to make money. I did. I had a picture in my head in terms of the type of career that I wanted to have. I wanted to be positioned in a high-profile career and live the lifestyle that goes along with that, which wasn't so far off from my parents' vision for me. I wasn't trading-off financial success for the path that was less mainstream. I just knew I needed to be successful in an area that was going to inspire me.

This quote by Howard Thurman really resonates with me:

> "Don't ask yourself what the world needs. Ask yourself what makes you come alive, and go do that, because what the world needs is people who have come alive."

I've always believed you should follow what you really believe in. Follow your passion. If a person is five feet tall with a passion for being an NBA player, that might not happen. But then again, there have been some 5'3" NBA players. There aren't many, but they do exist. Passion alone isn't enough–there are certain things that you'll need to have in place.

If you have the skills that suggest you can be good at something and you're passionate about it, why not? I think that works. Like I said, it took my father a while to acknowledge that I'd made a good choice, because he didn't get it. He'd say, "How are you going to make any money doing that HR stuff?" I had to be convinced of it as an adult before I could convince him. Still, it was probably six or seven years before he fully accepted that I really knew what I was doing.

People often think you have to focus on what will make money first in order to be a personal or financial success. I think the person who's the best at anything they love will make money. Again, "make money" is a relative term. What does that really mean? Once I decided I wanted to develop expertise in this space, the idea of being a consultant came into play, and it became clear that there were paths I could take and be financially successful in this space.

Everyone has the right to envision what they want to do for work, and that should encompass the way you want to live and the kind of lifestyle you want to have. Do you want to travel? Do you want to be more local? Do you want to impact people's lives? Do you want to make lots of money? Do you want to have flexibility with your lifestyle? Do you want to spend time with your kids? Those are all personal questions that we each have to answer, and as you find your personal passions, you'll want to decide how you can take them and turn them into something that allows you to meet those needs.

If you like to cook, you can be a chef. You could work at a diner, or you could own a chain of restaurants. You could work for the rich and famous, like Rachel Ray. She was Oprah Winfrey's personal chef before getting her own television show and line of cookware. You could write cookbooks, go into restaurant marketing/PR, work at a food publication, or be a reality show or YouTube superstar. All of those possible careers are centered on cooking, but each of those options will deliver very different lifestyles and different potential financial outcomes.

You'll want to look at that passion and figure out how you will turn it into something that will allow you to live a lifestyle that's aligned with what you want to do. Don't just ask yourself "How much money do I want to make?" Ask yourself, "What kind of lifestyle do I see myself having that allows me to make money, have freedom, and be happy?"

I say "having freedom" because one of the other currencies that younger people are looking for when they map out their career is flexibility and freedom. I think many people from my generation and the Baby Boomer generation traded-off flexibility and freedom for financial stability. So, many of us said, "I'm going to work for this company and dedicate my time and work my 10-12 hours a day and travel when I'm told to travel or move when I'm told to move, and in return I'll have certain security."

That was the Baby Boomer model, and it began to break down as businesses started right-sizing and changing some of the financial promises that corporations had historically provided to their employees. These days, I'm finding many young people want to make money, because you need money to buy things in this world, but they also want their freedom and the flexibility to call some of their own shots. More and more, Boomers are envying this flexibility and looking for it as they pursue second and third careers.

Make it tangible

I was blessed in the sense that I got some of my early work experiences very early. I had my first tangible work experience in corporate America at the age of 14. I'll talk about that more later, but that experience showed me what I liked and what I didn't like as a potential career, and I was able to make adjustments in what I chose next. So, as a freshman in college, when I saw an organizational leadership program being offered, it wasn't hypothetical to me. I knew that I was attracted to it because I'd witnessed organizational dynamics at work in the corporations where I had interned. I said to myself, "I think I could influence this."

The challenge is how to take what you think you want to do and make it tangible as quickly as possible. You want to learn about publishing? Why not publish something? You want to learn about writing? Why not write something? You want to learn about consulting? Again, why don't you consult on something?

For example, when I was in college, I created a little leadership consulting business, complete with business cards. (In fact, I got into trouble because I didn't realize that I wasn't supposed to use the Purdue logo on my business cards, when I was a student there. No harm done, and I filed it away under experience.) I had decided that I liked the experience I was getting in my internships and I wanted to position myself to deliver and sell it, to enable others.

So, by the time I graduated from college, it was easy to

make the leap to something bigger.

Your experiences in life teach you about yourself

When I was a kid in Albany, GA, my brother and I integrated the school there. We were the first black family to move into this particular neighborhood, which my parents had chosen because it had the best school. Education was big in my family, so that's where I went.

But beyond the school curriculum, I got a much bigger education on race relations in the South. Sure, I have stories about getting into fights and being called names, but what lingers with me is the memory of one particular substitute teacher, an older retired gentleman. We'll call him Mr. Edwards.

I still remember his face. He was a frequent substitute, the kind the kids got to know over the years because he would be at the school quite often when a teacher was sick or couldn't come in. And because I saw him so often and perhaps because I was an A student, we were friendly, and we would laugh a lot. He was very nice to me.

Until he wasn't.

It was toward the end of the sixth grade, about two weeks left before school was out. I guess I had become too familiar with Mr. Edwards - too comfortable - and I must have responded to one of his jokes in a way that went against the traditional racial norms of the South.

I'll never forget this, because he called me aside, and he said, "You know, Orlando, you need to know something. You're smart. You're really smart, especially for a nigger. But you need to know that in this world, niggers don't amount to anything."

This wasn't the segregationist era of Jim Crow. This was 1980. And as a 12-year-old, to hear those words from someone I liked and trusted was shattering. Unfortunately, as a black young man in the Deep South, I'd had enough negative experiences to be accustomed to this kind of racism from strangers. But this was somebody who I thought was a friend. Even with all of our friendly bantering over the course of the year, he still thought there were rules, and I had broken them. He needed to put me back in my place.

He was an older man then, and it's been a long time. I'm sure he's gone by now. But I used the pain of that experience as a source of motivation through high school, college, and the early part of my career, and I thought of him often because I intended to prove him wrong. Sometimes negative experiences fuel vision and I used what happened to set out to prove without a doubt that I would amount to something.

When I was young, I was a really good artist. I could draw like nobody's business. I could take any photograph and draw it freehand. I really enjoyed drawing and was good at it, so I took art classes. I thought I wanted to make my living doing something in the artistic space. However, I was challenged by my father to leverage my math and science skills, and to do some things that would translate to a higher income. The thought of raising a struggling artist for the rest of his life wasn't exactly what my folks wished for me.

So, I did what a lot of kids do. I tried to combine the two: something artistic that I would enjoy, with something my folks wanted that would give me the security and income stream they wanted for me. I thought, maybe I wanted to be an engineer, and maybe I could design cars. (I've always liked cars.) Or, maybe I could be an architect.

When I was in eighth grade, after we had moved back to New Jersey, I discovered that Bell Labs had a program called the Summer Technical Education Program, and I applied and was selected. Groups of students studied standard computer programming languages (at the time it was Basic and C++) during the summers of eighth and ninth grade. By the time I was entering my sophomore year in high school, I had been chosen as one of the six or seven students to have internships with them. By then, I had ambitions to do something in the computer science, technology, or engineering spaces.

My very first internship was where my first 'aha' moment with people dynamics–my eventual course of college study–really took place. The guy I worked for then was really smart. He was also a nice, funny and a good mentor. I learned a lot from him, and I noticed that when *his* boss (the vice president of the department) came into the room, his behavior and demeanor would change completely. He'd get nervous and fidgety. He couldn't talk well or express his ideas, and he didn't really show well. As a 15-year-old kid and a junior in high school, I saw both of them as just older guys than me. But clearly there was something about the one guy that made the other guy less productive.

At the end of that summer I had the opportunity to talk to my boss's boss. He asked me how my summer was, how the internship was going, and if I was enjoying the experience. I was, and I told him about how great it was, how much I'd learned, and what a great boss I had. Then I said, "I don't know if you noticed, but my boss is really smart and does really good stuff. He's a really good teacher for me, but you make him really nervous. When you come into the room, he doesn't come off as smart as he really is."

I didn't realize it at the time, but that was my first organizational development (OD) intervention. He acted intrigued and surprised by this (I was only 15, after all) and he asked for some examples, which I shared with him. He thanked me for the insight and said he would think about how to deal with my manager differently.

Several years later, I was studying engineering at Purdue, a great engineering school. At Purdue they also had a small program called Organizational Leadership and Supervision (it's now called Technology, Leadership, and Innovation).

With fewer than 100 students in it at the time, the program was essentially the study of organizational dynamics, leadership, corporate structures, and organizational development. It focused on issues like: How do you maximize your corporation, your structure, your leadership, your team, in order to derive the most value and impact by your people? That social engineering aspect, the people dynamics I saw, was exciting. I thought back to my early internship experiences and realized it wasn't the technical engineering work that excited me, it was more about the engineering of the environment of the people. When I discovered that major, it really clicked for me, and it became very clear what I wanted to do with my career. I made the decision halfway through my freshman year that this was what I wanted to do.

Let your vision guide you

As you think about your career, you'll want to begin with a point of view, a picture, and answer to the question: "Where do you want to be in 10 years?" If you haven't asked yourself this question, you should. Career planning starts with a vision.

Maybe you remember the 80s television show, *L.A. Law*. It focused on a group of power-player lawyers, including a headstrong attorney named Jonathan Rollins, played by Blair Underwood. He was the only African American on the show, and he played that character for eight years. He was a young, good-looking guy with power suits and a briefcase, a little bit of attitude, a confident approach, and big energy.

That was the picture I had in my head of who I wanted to be when I was envisioning my career. I wanted authority, and for people to look up to me. I wanted to command attention and deliver advice and counsel--things that clients would be willing to pay for. Instead of pursuing law I became a consultant, but for me the outcome was the same.

It's important to have a picture or a vision of what you

choose for your career. It doesn't have to be fully rendered, but you should have a point of view about how you want your life to be, how you want your career to be, and how you want to be positioned in the world.

And I understand that other factors may be at play in terms of peoples' perception of you. I'm a 6'4", 230-pound African American male. When I walk into a room, often the initial assumption isn't that I might be a corporate executive, a lawyer, or a doctor. More often, perceptions lead people to other conclusions such as: "He looks like a professional athlete," although I'm growing out of this one as I get older. Now they ask, "Who'd you play for back in the day?" or "I bet he's a bodyguard or limo driver." My physical attributes are where their impression of me starts, and it's been this way my whole life. I've had to learn how to move people away from preconceived notions and closer to the truth.

In 2010, I was working in New York City. At the time, I drove a Mercedes S600, the big-body Mercedes that oftentimes limo drivers use, particularly in New York. On Thursdays and Fridays in the city, it was particularly hard to catch a cab after work. So, frequently people would try to find a limo driver who was free and see if he would be willing to give them a lift. Remember, this was before Uber and Lyft.

One Thursday evening, I was sitting at a stoplight in my car listening to jazz on the radio. A guy came up to my car and knocked on the window, and I heard him say, "Hey, you want a fare to LaGuardia?" Without even waiting for a response, he opened the door, threw in his bag, and got in.

At that moment, my dual degrees from Purdue University, my awards for outstanding performance, my articles and job title–even the shirt and tie I was still wearing, having just left work–all went out the window. What he saw was a forty-something African American in an expensive car, and he apparently assumed the only way I could be driving it was as a limo driver.

I was pretty angry. I turned to him and used some colorful words, and he realized his mistake. He jumped out of the car and ran, but it ruined my day. Heck, it ruined my week. In fact, I still freshly recall this story to this day. It's something that really affected me.

Now, there is nothing wrong with being a limo driver. Please don't miss my point. But why the assumption that I was a limo driver? Some might ask, "Well, couldn't this mistake happen to anyone--including a white person?" And to that I would answer, "Sure, but has it happened to anyone you know who isn't a person of color?"

This isn't a book on race and, sure, there will be examples of mistaken assumptions of this nature that have been made with white people. The problem is that for Black folks, these stories are not rare, or exceptions to the rule. I could tell you dozens of stories where my race drove a perception of how I was viewed on the street or in the workplace, and it's true for literally every Black person I know. I am Black. It's part of who I am. So, I have to manage it because others make decisions and assumptions based on their own biases.

It's human nature. People start with a set of perceptions that may not position you well for what you want to do. So, how do you manage the reputation that you build and the image that you try to portray? It's an important question, and it's why I say, for all people, but particularly for people of difference, the details are particularly important. Your clothes, the stories you tell, the experiences that you pursue. They all play into your image, into the opportunities that are presented to you, and into your ability to achieve the things to which you aspire.

> "Build your own dreams, or someone else will hire you to build theirs."
>
> –Farrah Gray

What are your unique characteristics that elicit reactions from others?

Whether it's right, wrong, or indifferent, perceptions matter, and you can't bet that you'll have the same luck or opportunity as someone else if all things were equal–because they aren't. Even if you do get all the details right–for example, you're wearing a suit and look polished--you still might be mistaken for a limo driver.

It's worth repeating. Perceptions matter, and this book is

about how you prepare yourself to maximize your potential. If you are a member of any minority population, you have to start with your desired perception in mind. If biases don't naturally position you well for what you want to do, the reputation you build becomes even more critical. For all people, and especially people of color, all of these things–perception, attitude, and image–play into how people perceive and respond to you. You might not think it's fair, and it's often not. But perceptions don't have to hold you back or keep you down. It's true for everyone.

Envisioning your future, the inaugural principle, is the first step toward how you position yourself for opportunities and how others perceive you. Now, onto successfully preparing you for the corporate world . . .

"For tomorrow belongs to the people who prepare for it today."

—African Proverb

CHAPTER 2

Prepare for the Corporate World

Building your skills and professional capabilities is critical

You can't succeed without being good at what you do. Once you're good at what you do, you need to have the ability to take credit for it, and then you can monetize it. That's why this all starts with the question: Do you have a passion for what you do? Publishing, photography, the bar business? Your passion fuels your career. What is it you love doing?

I told you about my friend who wants to own a bar. In fact, he more than enjoys it, he's passionate about the bar business, and he's good at it. He wants to connect his bartending skills to the lifestyle he wants. He wants more income and a say in how the bar is run, how it's branded, and so on. He wants to actually own a bar, taking what he loves about bartending, and clicking it up to the next level. He's trying to figure out how to do that.

But what he has now is knowledge about bartending. He doesn't have knowledge about bar ownership and the things that it will take to successfully own a bar, and this is where people fail. They have a skill set, a resource of knowledge, an expertise they love and enjoy–all which have value and at which they excel. But that's only one piece.

The second piece may even be as important as the first: continuing to grow that passion and expand your skills to include what it takes to own, operate, run, or sustain your own business. Successful entrepreneurs like to keep their skills fresh and improving. Once you discover your passion, you have to learn how to take that passion and click it up. You need to figure out how to monetize it and do better and different things with it.

Maybe you're a great chef. But, how do you stand out as a great chef? Do you create a cooking show? A reality television show? A cooking school? Do you write a book? Work for celebrities? How do you click up what you love doing to a place where it's truly your dream career? It may be C-suite level status or having your own business. There are no right or perfect answers–only the dream you have envisioned for yourself. You really can have the dream job, if you can envision it and then kickstart the second principle of preparing for the corporate world.

Transitioning mid-career

Let me tell you about Genevie Kocourek, who became a doctor at age 59. An information technology director who led rock-climbing trips in her spare time, she decided to take a wilderness first-responder course to learn how to care for injured climbers. Although her high school guidance counselor had discouraged her from becoming a doctor when she was young, her early passion for medicine was reignited while taking this course. Not only was she rediscovering her love of medicine, but she was learning about it in 38-degree weather, in the rain, and still loving every minute of it.

With her passion reignited, she learned that her employer was offering early retirement, so she and her husband did some research, considered the options and made a plan. Genevie took early retirement, went to medical school, and graduated – becoming a doctor at age 59.

Genevie didn't jump ship the moment her vision became a plausible future. She began by exploring what it would take for her vision to succeed. She and her husband met with a financial advisor to map out the economic aspects of medical school and decided that she would take one or two classes each semester to fulfill her pre-med requirements while she continued to work. They asked her 81-year old mother, who already lived with them, to help out with cooking meals. When she finally entered med-school she lived in the dorms on campus at the University of Wisconsin and came home on weekends. She broke her vision down into executable steps, held herself accountable with her family, and got it done.

The lesson we learn from Genevie is important. When I ask people "What do you want to be when you grow up," I get answers like "Successful" or "Rich," and I say, "What does that really mean?" You have to break your ambitions down to enough specificity that they are actionable. If they aren't actionable, you can't hold yourself accountable for getting them done.

And I know other people who have made the shift to new careers that they were passionate about. For example:

Lauren Imparato, a Princeton graduate and a hedge-fund manager for Morgan Stanley, quit her job after seven years to open a yoga studio. She completely changed her career trajectory toward something she was personally passionate about.

Jonathan Fields almost died from an ulcer that landed him in the emergency room at the height of his career as a New York City attorney. That unfortunate wake-up call motivated him to transition from being a high-strung lawyer to a yoga teacher and health club owner. He went on to write several best-selling books and became a speaker as well.

Genevie, Lauren and Jonathan aren't odd or isolated case studies. Millions of men and women are turning their passions into a second (or third) profession. For many of those doing so now, they're pursuing careers in fields they never even knew existed when they were starting out as young professionals. But they followed their passions, they made a plan, and they made the change.

Age is just a number. You may move more slowly than you did in your 20s, but you have the skills, and the mental and emotional wisdom, that more than make up for the speed.

For many midlife career professionals, even the idea of continuing to do what they've been doing for 20, 30, or 40 years makes them want to cry. But understand this: It's not only okay to change career paths when you realize you no longer love what you're doing, it's strongly advised. Just ask Jonathan Fields. His law career almost killed him. The stress and demands of working in a career or job you don't love can cut your life expectancy short. Studies have shown that moving or transitioning into a new career can literally be a lifesaver in terms of mental and physical health.

> You won't be alone in your decision. If you are not certain how to fund yourself through this transition toward your dream career, there are plenty of organizations that exist to help.

Look at the worst-case scenario

Something I've always done when assessing an opportunity is to look at the worst-case scenario. If I can live with the worst case, then it's easy to jump in. Most people look for the best case, such as: "If I do this, I'll be a millionaire and that'll be great." But, if it fails and you're going to significantly impact your professional momentum or personal well-being, then maybe you should reconsider.

So, ask yourself, what's the worst-case scenario? Because, if you can live with the worst-case scenario, then it's easy to take the risk, and you can jump in with both feet, knowing you can handle the worst while driving toward the best outcome.

There are some truths about executives, particularly senior executives, and their ability to make decisions quickly and with confidence that they'll be able to handle the consequences. Senior executives tend to be comfortable with being wrong and then adjusting those decisions if they must. Being a successful C-suite executive is not about being right, it's about managing when you're wrong. Because, inevitably, you are going to be wrong. You're going to make some mistakes. It's impossible to be perfect.

Know your boundaries and follow your values

People who work really hard to get to the C-suite want to be invited into the tent, to be one of the small cadre of folks who are running a large asset. But, not every invitation into the tent is a good invitation. You have to ask yourself, "What do I have to trade in order to be accepted?"

Once, a senior leader who I admired at a former company took me aside and said, "Orlando, we like what you're doing. We think you could be a great asset to this firm. But sometimes you need to lie, steal, and cheat a little bit in order to win, and we just want to make sure you're willing to do whatever it takes in order to win." They were asking, basically, "Are you willing to play some of the dirty pool that we're playing in order to sit at this table?"

I will tell you, in that situation, my resumé was on the street the next day because dirty pool is a short-term answer. It would have been exciting to be a part of that leadership team, but the trade-off wasn't worth it to me.

It turned out to be the right call. That company ended up having a number of leadership, financial, and ultimately, company valuation issues within a couple of years.

Another time, I had a boss tell me I was too nice, and that I needed to be more ruthless in my management style. But the word ruthless just doesn't fit in my value system. It's not something I believe in as a management style. You can be tough, you can be more assertive, you can be aggressive at times, but ruthless is not my word. So, if that was required in order to be on that team, then I couldn't be on that team.

More recently, I was exploring an opportunity with a company during a period of civil unrest across the U.S. in reaction to the George Floyd murder at the hands of police. I had written an opinion piece in reaction to the protests, based on my own experience, and had posted it to a popular social media channel.

After the post, I received a call from the search firm who said that while the company was really excited about me joining the firm, if I were asked to join I'd have to stop posting any opinion pieces on race relations in this country and "fly under the radar."

I thought to myself, does he really think that during a time when so much has been happening with the police and African Americans, that I'm not going to have a voice? As a Black person in a position of leadership, I feel it is my responsibility to share my perspective on issues of race and social justice in this country. And if he was willing to ask this of me now, during the interview phase, I had concerns about what it would be like if I took the role.

I had to ask myself, do I turn this job down out of concern that my voice will be muffled on these types of issues, or do I pursue this company as a great opportunity and use it as a chance to teach about the positive impact that diversity can bring to an organization and to business?

I share this story because many of you may one day also be faced with a situation where you are asked to make a similar choice. So whether you're Black or Brown, a woman, LGBTQ, differently-abled, or a member of any other community that our society considers diverse, you may have to decide how you blend those interests with how you work, particularly as you make your way up the corporate ladder.

> The point is this: to prepare for the corporate world, it's important you have a clear picture of what work you want to do and what you stand for.

Being true to your authentic self will serve you well in the long run. What you want to do should not trump your principles. In order for you to have a sustainable career, it's important to be clear of this inside your own head and heart.

Preparing for the corporate world

There are a lot of ways to learn in life and sitting in a classroom listening to an instructor is only one of them. I encourage learning one-on-one and ask everyone you meet about something they do that interests you.

Talk to everyone you come in contact with who is in your field of interest about their job, what they do, and what they love about it. You can learn a lot in ten minutes. Learn to listen and be interested in people. Offer to buy someone a cup of coffee and say, "May I ask you a couple questions?"

Mentors often appear where you least expect them. The very first day of my high school internship, my manager invited me into his office and placed a half-filled glass of water on his desk.

He said, "So, Orlando, I want to welcome you to the company. This is your first day here. What is this here on my desk?"

I answered, "It's a glass of water."

"Nope," he said. "This represents the company. Take your finger and put it in the glass. What do you have now?"

I'm sure I gave him a goofy look and I put my finger in the glass. "Uhh…a glass of water with my finger in it," I said.

"No, this is still the company. Welcome. Today's your first day on the inside. Now, pull your finger out. What's the difference?"

I answered, "Well, there really isn't any."

He said, "Exactly. No difference. Always remember that."

His first lesson to me was that this is a large corporation and people are expendable. In a corporate environment, you are dispensable. Whether you're here or you're not here, the company moves on, and it's still pretty much intact.

I thought it was an interesting lesson that I've always managed as I've worked my career. These are large systems. You want to have an impact, but the only thing you own is the experience you get from that company, because that company can–and will--move on without you. People often fail to realize that they will be more impacted by the company than the company is by them.

Later on, I had another internship with a large pharmaceutical company and I'll never forget my manager there. He was short and kind of round, and he had a beard. He seemed to be stuck in middle management, never getting promoted to the upper levels. He used to always say to me, "Oh, Orlando, you're going to get far. You're tall and good-looking."

My manager was a smart guy, an engineer, and he'd been around for more than 20 years. I thought he was just being nice to me because I was a kid. But, over the course of the summer, I realized this guy was one of the smartest people there.

He said, "Look, the only reason I'm still here is because I have 20-something patents, and I've accomplished a lot for the company in that time. But I don't have the looks to get upstairs." This was a regular theme of his… insisting there is a look one needs to be promoted to the C-suite, and he didn't have it because he was short, overweight, and had a beard. I don't know how true it was for him directly, but he felt it was true and that's what mattered. It impacted how he presented himself to the world.

I also knew that I needed to think about how to dress and present myself. As I worked for different companies, I'd pay attention: How did the people who worked upstairs look? Was there a C-suite look or a corporate executive look? Did I have it, or could I create my own version of it?

If you're interested in breaking into the C-suite level, there are number of things you're going to need to succeed.

- **A STELLAR PERFORMANCE RECORD:** First and foremost you have to put together a track record of success. Everyone who aspires to those levels is smart, delivers, and has had impact throughout their lives and careers. They have a track record of things they can point to that have been significant.

You can't buy, sell, or trade that record. It's proof you've been tried by fire and succeeded. Remember to write down your accomplishments along the way. It's easy to forget when a boss recognizes you on the company intranet or a customer writes a glowing thank you letter. Snap a pic and write your triumphs down.

• **A STRONG BRAND:** Getting things done, even done fast, done well, and done in spite of all odds, is great, but you also want to spend time investing in your brand so when people hear your name they know immediately that you're that person who gets things done. Your reputation or brand is a lot of what a company is buying when they hire you. You'll hear things like, "Bring so-and-so in. They're going to have an impact." Especially if the C-suite is your ambition; you need to spend some time early on thinking about your corporate brand. You can't build a brand overnight. You start by making contributions toward it over the course of your career.

• **A STRONG NETWORK:** The difference between middle management and the C-suite revolves a lot around relationships. That's something you've got to invest time in. It's a trade-off. You're trading-off spending time with friends, family, and children in exchange for developing relationships related to your career.

You may not be able to go to your child's school or sporting events because you're going to dinner, or a networking event, or on golf trips, or whatever you need to do in order to create relationships. It's a hard call when it comes to family, friends and time because there's not a clear line. And unfortunately, building a network isn't about going to a networking event and exchanging business cards, and the next day you're called in for the big job. You may invest in events and people for years before the relationships pay off.

And for people who didn't grow up with parents or role models in the C-suite, this frame of mind may be a challenging transition. Because working hard isn't enough to get to the C-suite; you have to think like an executive, not line staff. These people may buy the idea of being smart and delivering, but they sometimes don't understand the part about creating a strong brand and a strong, diverse network. They don't invest enough time in something where they can't see tangible results.

• **AN ABILITY TO COLLABORATE:** I believe in the concept of "collective intelligence," the notion that if we leverage the brain power of the group we will win as a company. None of us is as smart individually as we are together. There is a collective intelligence network in every organization, but the power comes in the ability to harness it. This is done through collaborative leaders. Here, these leaders are able to tap into the minds and hearts of their employees and pull out the best, new ideas and commit to getting those ideas turned into successful new products and services.

• **A CAN-DO ATTITUDE:** Life isn't fair. It turns on everyone, hurts everyone, and ruins a lot of relationships, projects, and jobs. I don't know of a person alive today who hasn't said, "That's not fair," at some point in their lives. Somehow it feels better–at least briefly–when you can stand around the water cooler and complain about how unfair life is, or how someone did you wrong. If you fall into that whine and complain mode too much, you can write off any chance at getting into the C-suite. Attitude is everything.

When you're a leader, you spot what's wrong, but you address it, fix it, change it, or improve it. You don't blame, whine, or complain. You act. You may not think people notice, but they do. That's why no matter what happens, "you never let them see you sweat," and don't complain about what has happened. You acknowledge it, smile, and address it. If it's a problem, you solve it. And, you do it all while remaining positive, upbeat, professional, and confident about it, no matter what.

• **BEING DEPENDABLE:** Dependability may sound boring, but it's the most critical of all workplace skills. When you're dependable, your co-workers and supervisors learn they can trust you to deliver. This makes you not only likable, but promotable. If you're dependable, you require less supervision and control and are more likely to be counted on for a new opportunity. When co-workers see they can trust you to deliver on time, every time, they are inspired to do the same.

Management sees those who are dependable as someone

more likely to be a good manager. If layoffs or downsizing are in the works, dependable employees are the last to be laid off because fewer people are doing the same number of jobs and management wants to ensure the work gets done. When you're a consistent member of the team, you build on your brand. Dependability means you're more likely to get higher visibility assignments and to be seen by higher management. So, what makes a person dependable? Several elements that make up dependability:

o **Good organizational skills:** It's hard to deliver on time, every time, when you can't manage your time, your organizational methods, or your calendar. Find a calendar and time tracking program (paper or digital) that you like and enjoy using. It doesn't have to be complex or have a lot of bells and whistles. It does have to work for you. It does need to be able to help you list, find and organize your life and projects. If you don't like it, you won't use it, so find a good notebook, calendar, or app that will help you get and stay organized. Organizational skills mean you're able to make and keep lists and keep track of what has been done and what needs to be done. Having the ability to break down a project into chunks, and to ensure each task is accomplished in the proper order so other tasks can be completed, is rare. It's also extremely valuable.

o **Good work ethic:** Can you finish a task even when you're bored, tired, or tempted by other diversions? Can you finish a task and finish it well even if it doesn't seem important? A strong work ethic involves being responsible, having a desire to do a good job whether or not anyone else is watching or checking on your work. A good work ethic means you have integrity and a sense of pride in your work. Quality is important, both in your actions and the finished product.

o **Trustworthy:** Integrity and trust are strongly lacking in today's workforce. Being a man or woman of your word is important. Your supervisors and co-workers must know you won't steal, lie, or cheat and that you are honest and keep your promises. Even if the news is bad, can you be trusted to deliver it?

o **Ability to delegate:** Being dependable means being able to deliver, or get a job done. It doesn't necessarily mean you have to do the entire job yourself. Finding people you can delegate to–dependable people–is how leaders get things done. When you do reach the C-suite, you're going to need to be able to identify other dependable people and know how to delegate tasks to them to ensure you deliver the projects you've promised.

o **Disciplined:** It takes a strong person to stick to a task when they're tired, bored, hungry, sleepy, or distracted. Discipline is what keeps dependable people dependable. A disciplined person can stick to a task and finish it no matter what the distractions or challenges. It's not an easy skill to develop, but it's invaluable when you have it.

Thirty years out

None of us really knows where we'll be in one year let alone 10, 20, or 30 years. That's OK. Visualize as clear a picture as you can for your next goal, knowing it will likely change. Start with where you want to be five years from now. Are you traveling? Who are you working for? What are you doing? Are you married? Do you have kids, a house? Think long and hard about what that picture looks like. Then ask yourself, what's the first executable step, or collection of steps, you can take to get that started?

Those answers come from talking to people, reading books, listening to people on TV and the internet, asking people questions, testing ideas. The more you explore and talk to other people, the more you learn and the more diverse your options become. Coming out of college, I wanted to work in consulting. Did I want to work in a really well-branded corporation? I asked a number of people and got conflicting answers. Some thought I should go into consulting; some thought I should go work for a really big brand. I collected all that data and then I made my own choice. Consulting. And by the time I did, I felt like I was pretty well informed and was convinced I'd made the right choice.

Once I decided what I wanted to do and where I wanted to go, I tried to execute that step as aggressively as I could. When you're managing your career, all answers are right, and all answers are wrong. I could have just as easily gone and worked for a corporation, and I'm sure I would have been successful. Because, as you go along, you figure it out. What's important is that you take in as much information as you need, and then go execute your decision.

And, if the path you choose isn't what you expected or wanted, then you can decide to do something else. Even if it ultimately ends up being wrong for you, that doesn't mean it was a wasted decision--we always learn from our decisions. When you are ready to change, then just change. That collection of learnings, miracles, and mistakes is how you grow. You learn from the things that didn't work well and prepare for the opportunities that avail themselves afterward. That's how to build a life and a career.

Must-have social skills

Education is the acquisition of knowledge–and experience is also an education. In other words, you learn by doing and you gain both experience and education by actually doing what it is you want to know. Along with the nuts and bolts of the job itself, there is another kind of experience and education you won't see in many textbooks. That is your social skill set, meaning, learning the psychology and people skills, also called "soft skills" of being a leader. These skills will actually take you farther than the hard skills alone. Even if you're a genius engineer, accountant, or lawyer, if you don't know how to interact well with people, network, communicate, engage, motivate, and show respect and appreciation for customers, clients, and co-workers, it won't really matter. So, learn and apply these skills.

And don't think you've arrived once you learn these. Never stop learning; never stop improving.

Here are people skills to prepare you for a corporate career–in less time and with more results.

• **LEARN PEOPLE'S NAMES:** Nothing is sweeter to anyone than the sound of their own name. Learn people's names and use the name in conversation. Greet people by name. Say goodbye using their name. Instead of "Talk to you later," say "Talk to you later, Brian." Use their name during your conversation, particularly if you're in a conversation with more than one person. Not only does this increase their value in the eyes of others listening, it signals a relationship and a connection. Don't shrug and say, "I'm bad with names." You remember the names of your current friends, right? By repeating a person's name when they're introduced, and then a couple of times during the conversation, you'll soon be able to remember names. When introduced to someone find a connection with the name. "Hi, David. Nice to meet you. David, eh? That's the name of my favorite high school coach. Did you play sports, David?"

• **BE RESPECTFUL OF EVERYONE:** From the people in the cafeteria, to the receptionist, to those in middle management, and even the kids of employees you happen to meet, be respectful. You never, ever know who is related to whom, whether dating, neighbors, or colleagues.

For example: In late January 2018, we had Oprah Winfrey and Gayle King on our soon-to-be inaugurated new ship, Nieuw Statendam, for a 3-day "Girls' Getaway Cruise." More than 2,000 women (and about 50 brave men) sailed with us to the Bahamas for a few days of bonding and fun.

On the day when the guests were boarding, I was standing in the gangway greeting everyone as they came aboard when I noticed two women standing by the elevators looking confused. They noticed me and the older one called me over. She showed me her key and ask how they might get to their stateroom. They had several big suitcases with them, so rather than find a free crewmember to assist, I offered to just take them up to their stateroom myself. When we reached the room, the woman with the key brought out her wallet and extracted a dollar from it, offering it to me as what I assumed was a tip.

I told her, "No thank you, ma'am, I work for the company and I don't expect a tip."

She asked, "Well, what do you do?"

Not wanting to make them feel awkward, I said, "I am in senior management."

She asked, "Senior management, what exactly is your job?"

I wasn't going to be able to avoid it any further, so I answered, "Well, I'm the president of the company, ma'am."

They both showed surprise and the second woman said,

"Auntie, you've got the president of the company carrying your bags! Wait until we tell our cousin!"

I wished them well and went on my way, as Oprah would soon be arriving at the ship and I wanted to be at the start of the gangway to greet her.

When Oprah's car arrived, I was there waiting for her on the red carpet among other senior leadership and ship officers. The passengers' door opened, and Oprah stepped out. I stepped forward to welcome her to the ship, and the first thing she says is, "I just heard the best story about you!"

Those ladies were Oprah's cousins.

Your reputation will always precede you. Always be kind and respectful.

Also, assume everything you say and do is being recorded (it often is) and posted to social media. When you respect everyone and connect with everyone, you build your brand. People will also return that respect and share information that helps you or keeps you from making a mistake. When I first started out in my career, I learned about my first promotion from the limo driver who was taking me to the airport. He had been driving me to the airport right after he had driven the president of the company.

He said, "Hey, Orlando. Congratulations on your new promotion!" He shared that he had heard this from the president and alluded to the fact that he had put in a good word for me. This taught me this lesson in a very powerful way. You never know who is going to be in a position to put in a good word for you, so make sure the only things they have to say are positive. Treat them with respect, share information when it is appropriate to do so, and thank them when they help you.

• **PICK YOUR BATTLES:** College is a transformative time for many young people, and it was definitely true for me. Two particular experiences at Purdue illustrate how adversity shaped my thinking about how to manage and interact with people. These lessons are things I've used often throughout my career.

On my very first day of college, my father dropped me off and helped me get settled into the dorms. The same day, I met another young man, Doug, who's still one of my best friends to this day. Doug was on my floor; he's African American, and we clicked instantly in the way that college freshmen do. There were five of us from that dorm who bonded pretty quickly that first weekend, all African American. Classes didn't start for a few days, so we went looking for girls, as young freshmen in college often do.

We were walking off campus near an apartment building when we spotted some young men–they happened to be white–who were out on the balcony with a keg, drinking beers. As the five of us walked under one of the apartment's balconies, one of the guys on the balcony yelled, "Why don't you monkeys go back to Africa, where you belong?"

I had been on campus for four hours—my father had dropped me off and he was already driving back to Jersey—and I had already been called a monkey. I remember turning to Doug, and I said, "I don't know about you, but I'm from Jersey, and where I'm from, those are fighting words." He turned to me and said, "I'm from the south side of Chicago. Let's go."

We made a beeline up to the apartment, and I banged on the door. "Come out here and call me that," I yelled.

Soon we heard sirens, and the police arrived and intervened. We had words and a major altercation was avoided, but the damage was done. After the police left, I called my mother and I said, "Ma, when Dad checks in, send him back. I'm not staying here." And I told her the story.

Understandably, she began to get upset, but I told her not to worry. I figured I would just get a bus ticket and go home. Maybe I could enroll in Rutgers.

Then she asked, "Can you just give me one semester? Stay that long, and if you hate it in December, you can come home and you don't have to go back."

I paused, and I said, "Okay, Ma. One semester. But I'm not staying here."

Her bet was that in those three months I would figure it out enough to stay, and I was convinced I wouldn't, but she won that bet. I got two degrees from Purdue, and some of my best friends and the best experiences of my life happened there. I had to figure it out, and I had to fight for it the whole year.

After I'd made it through that first semester, I went back for a second semester which started in the dead of winter. Purdue is located in West Lafayette, Indiana, and winters can get pretty cold. One night, I was walking home from the library in the snow and a car drove past. Someone from inside hit me with a snowball and called me the N-word. It was just one of those days. I was cold and tired, it had been a rough day, and I had no patience for getting hit by a snowball and being called the N-word.

So, I took off in a sprint after the car. It was like the first scene in that movie Bad Boys, where Will Smith chases a car on foot. I was trying to cut through cross-streets and catch the car at a light. I think there were two or three young men in the car, and I chased them for five minutes, which felt like thirty. I never caught the car, and I was pissed, angry, and hurt. This was an academically demanding school, and on top of it I had to deal with that kind of stuff. I called home with the intention of talking to my mother, but I ended up talking to my dad.

My dad said it was the best thing that ever happened to me, not catching that car. "If you'd caught them, and you'd beaten them up, you'd be the one getting kicked out of school. That's what they want. They want to disrupt you, and they want to get you off your path. Something you have to learn is that when people come at you and attack you, you'll have to discern between the people and events that are roadblocks to what you want to achieve, and the people and events that are not. If they're not roadblocks to what you want to achieve, you have to learn how to quickly get over them and only focus on the things that are keeping you from your goals."

If it's a teacher or somebody you're working with who is blatantly trying to prevent you from achieving your goals, that's when you have to fight. But there are also situations where it's best to control your anger and move on with your life.

That's probably one of the best pieces of life advice I've ever received, and I've used it over and over again.

- **HAVE A SENSE OF HUMOR:** Nothing defuses tension like a good sense of humor. If you don't have one, watch those who do, and figure out what makes them funny. No one likes to be the butt of a joke, and they'll remember you for a long time if your humor humiliates them or someone they like, so try to keep it positive. Dr. Maya Angelou was known to have said, "People will forget what you said. People will forget what you did. But people will never forget how you made them feel." She was right.

And in this day and age this should go without saying, but always avoid sarcasm and inappropriate sexual or racial jokes. Keep it clean, even with those you consider friends. You never know where or how far an off-color joke will travel, and that's really not something you ever want to have to worry about.

- **PROACTIVE PROBLEM SOLVING:** One of the things I've often heard and always practiced was to never complain about something I couldn't solve. Complaining about something you can't change only annoys you and those around you. If you must complain about a situation, policy, or practice, follow it up with at least one suggestion for a way to change it, if not three. Saying, "Why doesn't someone do something?" is not a solution. Don't whine. Children whine.

State your objection non-emotionally and then follow it with, "So I was thinking _______ might be a way we can make this work." If you can solve the problem without making a big deal of it, do that. Someone once moved a piece of non-essential equipment being stored in the copy room so that it faced a different direction. This freed up a couple of feet of space since the equipment was narrower that way. It also allowed the copier to be moved almost a foot over, which made it easier to access the light switch without getting copy machine toner on your arm while reaching behind the machine. No one took credit for it, they just did it. Be proactive. See a problem and solve it.

- **BE SUCCESSFUL AND LIKEABLE:** People want to work with or for people who they like, and they want those people to be successful. Andy Kazlow, a mentor and a friend to me, had a really big chief of human resources officer (CHRO) job--bigger than my CHRO job. One day a headhunter called me and said, "Hey, there's going to be a change at X company. The head of HR job is going to become available. Are you interested?"

I knew that company. In fact, that was my friend Andy's job. So, I immediately said, "Well, no. No, I don't want that job."

About a week later, I got a call from Andy, and he said, "Hey, has anybody called you about any particularly interesting jobs?" And I said, "Well, yes–actually, somebody called me about yours." And he said, "Why didn't you respond? Orlando, I sent them to talk to you. I'm going to be moving on and working on something different. I'm working on my replacement, and I sent them to you. You're my friend, you're good, and I want you to have this opportunity." I remember the way he said it, and it has always resonated with me. So, there is an element of the "need to be likeable" wherever you are in your career.

• **BE A DIPLOMAT**: Being able to calm people down, mitigate workplace drama, and relate to and understand those around you is a golden skill to have or develop. What's your people radar like? Can you sense and defuse hostility, anger, or frustration before it peaks and boils over in a group? Can you be patient and understanding with the office hothead without getting upset yourself? Upper management notices people skills like this and will consider you a valuable asset.

• **BE FLEXIBLE:** You're not the only person in the room. Being flexible, willing to accommodate others for the good of the team, or project and adapt, is a strength. Knowing when to be flexible and when to stand your ground is an even more valuable skill, but one that comes with time and experience.

• **DON'T TAKE YOURSELF TOO SERIOUSLY:** Try to create

environments where there is enjoyment along the way. Don't turn the workplace into one long party but make it a place where people enjoy going in the morning. Encounters with you should be something they look forward to, something that brightens their day and lifts their mood. Find moments to laugh with others, even about yourself. I can laugh with the guard, the assistant, the middle manager, and the CEO. The ability to share a laugh or a moment with anyone will be reflected with success in a career and success in life.

- **KEEP YOUR PROMISES:** Promises can be large or small. If you're talking to someone and make a casual promise, keep it or don't make it. It's very easy to say to a colleague, "I've just finished a great book on that very thing. I'll drop it by your office," and then forget. Don't wait for people to remind you of your promises. Write them down after you make them, and then keep them. Go back that very hour and write a note to yourself to put that book it in the mail, or give it to them personally, but keep your promise and keep it quickly. If you can't keep promises, don't make them. Don't even infer them.

Nothing hurts your brand or your reputation more than failing to keep a commitment or promise. If you can't attend a function or meeting, don't say, "I'll try to make it." Tell the person that you can't make it. If you want to attend and aren't sure you'll be able to, tell them you can't make it. Then if you can make it, do. They'll be pleasantly surprised, and they won't feel like you failed to deliver. When people hear, "I'll try," they take it as a promise. Never "try" to do anything. As Yoda said, "Try not. Do or do not. There is no try."

- **LEARN TO READ PEOPLE'S BODY LANGUAGE AND FACIAL EXPRESSIONS**: Body language, the non-verbal art of communication, was big in the 70s and 80s. It periodically rises to the top of people's awareness when a new book comes out, or there's a television show or movie where the skill is featured. From 2009 to 2011 much of the country was riveted by a television show called "Lie to Me." The show was based on the real-life skills and work of Dr. Paul Ekman, a psychologist who studied the science of human emotions and facial expressions. He has been called the best human lie detector in the business and has published several books on the art of facial reading. He also has online training to increase emotional awareness and detect deception. How good are you at reading expressions?

You don't have to become an expert but knowing how to spot the telltale signs of hesitancy, lies, confusion, anger, or boredom will go a long way to helping you learn to read and understand your clients, co-workers, and customers. Learning to read body language and facial expressions will help you see when a person is being honest or not. Strong body language and facial reading skills are invaluable if you are a negotiator, salesperson, manager, or work with people in any capacity. There are dozens of books on body language and Paul Ekman's site has even more resources and classes to help you. You can also begin simply by becoming a "people watcher" and becoming observant of how those around you act, talk, and move.

• **SHOW GOOD MANNERS:** Perhaps this quality, more than any other, will get you through almost any situation. Say "please" and "thank you." Send people thank you notes and cards. Show appreciation. Help out. If you weren't raised with a family who taught you how to act at dinners, parties, and meetings, or how to treat people well, then research online, read a book, or take a class. There are a variety of classes around the U.S. to teach executives the social skills they need to succeed.

John Malloy, author of "Live for Success," says that the final indicator of class in America was the possession of certain social skills. Of the 100 executives he surveyed while writing his book, 99 of them said that social skills were prerequisites to succeeding in business and social life. Manners are not a matter of just understanding what fork to use and what to say. Good manners are expressions of your attitude, not simply things you must do to conform.

Executive finishing schools and programs are available that teach a variety of skills for all kinds of situations, including business card protocol, golf etiquette, dining etiquette, deference, how to give a toast and so much more.

Remember, your education and experience is about becoming a whole person. It's about developing your brand and your communication skills as well as your job and management skills. The things you learn now will become the skills and habits you take into your career going forward. Choose them carefully and thoughtfully because they are the foundation for your career.

"Customers don't measure you on how hard you tried. They measure you on what you deliver."

–Steve Jobs

CHAPTER 3

Deliver Results

The third principle is the simplest yet most critical concept I can share for accelerating your career and nailing your desired place in Corporate America. In order to have success in your career you have to deliver results. Do you get things done? Is your work having a visible impact on the business? Delivering results is table stakes for a successful career. It is essential. If your answer to this question is no, there is no need to read any further.

> Having a long and successful career starts with having a reputation for delivering results.

When I advise people about their careers delivering results is where I start. If you want to eventually be in a position of leadership, you have to be able to draw a clear line between the work you do and its impact on the business. And if that line isn't clear or you can't define how your work supports the business, I recommend you look for a way to change jobs. It's imperative to position yourself as someone who gets things done and makes things better. That's the reputation that you want to have. Those are the people who get pulled into new opportunities and are promoted, especially early in one's career. During those formative years, delivering results is the fastest way to distinguish yourself from others in the organization. One way to think about work is to believe that if you do your job well, you'll get promoted. That may work some of the time, but that's inefficient thinking. A more reliable formula is when you can do the job of the person above you, that is when you'll get promoted.

A former boss would tell me, "If you think of your job as a box, you want to do work outside of your box and to make it bigger. That's how you expand your impact." I agree with this concept. When I was a young manager, I used to frequently ask my boss, "What are your top priorities? What are you working on?" Once I understood my boss's needs and issues, I simply added some of those things to my plate.

Think about it. If your friend showed up at your house unprompted and did your dishes, cleaned your house, and did your laundry, they'd probably stand out from your other friends.

You'd wonder what was wrong with them, but you'd let them in and do your chores. Over time, you'd become more dependent on them, and you'd eventually start looking for them to show up and do the dishes and laundry. Ultimately, you'd get to the point where you'd be disappointed on the days they didn't come. You'd miss the impact they had on your life by making your workload easier.

You get my point. It's a powerful way to position yourself at work. Develop a reputation for being a work killer. Someone who gets things done.

Are you a work killer? How do you know if this is the case for you?

My father worked really hard. He was the first one in the office and often the last one out. He'd come home and have dinner, and then put in a few more hours. There was no question my father was a work killer and it made for a long career for him. Coming in early and staying late is a good work ethic, but in today's work world, I don't think that's enough, or even necessary. You want to be brutally honest with yourself about the value of your work. It's important to work hard but working hard on things that are less important to the organization won't deliver the results you want from your career. If you want to understand the impact of your work, ask yourself these questions:

- Does your job deliver or promote revenue for the business? How?

- Does your job create or enable key products or services, or support customers? How?

- When there is a problem are you a "go to" person?

- If there was a need to reduce headcount by 20 percent, would your role/department survive? Why do you feel that way?

You need to have a very honest discussion with yourself in answering these questions. It would also be a good conversation to have with your personal Board of Directors (we'll discuss later in Chapter 7). If it's difficult to answer these questions or the answers are fuzzy for you, you might need to go back to the first principle and envision your future. In order to maximize your career trajectory, it's imperative that you are known for delivering results.

The lesson at Motorola

In 2002 I was made a partner at Delta Consulting in New York City. The youngest partner at Delta, by all accounts. I was on a great trajectory there. But in 2004, I was given the opportunity to head organizational development for the handset division at Motorola, and while things were going in a great direction with Delta, I really felt like I could have an impact on this American icon of a company, which at that time was in dire straits.

Three weeks into working with Motorola, I was part of one of the most dysfunctional meetings of my career. It started at 7 a.m. and lasted until about 8 p.m., and the range of topics we covered were all over the map - strategy, staffing, new product development, sales, and so on. I remember thinking that I may very well have made a mistake in taking the job. In the midst of this meeting, we had a presentation from the head of engineering, and he showed us a clay rendition of what would be known as the "Razor phone." He passed around this prototype of what he said would be the world's slickest phone, and everyone in the room became very excited. There was a lot of energy around this, so I was pretty surprised when the leadership team commenced to cancel the project right there in the meeting. They thought it was too expensive, too new, and too distinct from the existing products they had in place, so they decided not to pursue the product.

Later that day, I was walking down the hall with the president of the division, and he asked me how I was doing. Now, I've always tried to be very transparent, and if you ask me a question, I will answer it. So, I told him it was one of the more dysfunctional meetings I've ever participated in, and the one thing that everyone was excited about the executive leadership team had cancelled. With a puzzled look on this face, he asked me what I would recommend, and I told him I'd give him a recommendation the next day.

The next morning, I slid three pieces of paper across the table to him. Each was a detailed definition of a governance process: one for the staff meeting, one for new product development, and one for the strategic planning process. They were each very detailed–who would participate in each process, tentative agendas, the schedules, etc. He asked how it would work and I told him that I would be happy to manage it for him. And that's when I became the "governance czar" for the organization for all three of these processes.

One of the first things we did was re-tool the product development part of our process to fund "big bets" and innovations that better position our organization for the future, and it turns out, the very first big bet that we placed was the Razor Phone. The team developed and marketed it heavily, and very quickly it became the hottest phone in the world. It completely changed the financial trajectory of the company, with Motorola's stock going from $6 a share to $26 a share in one year.

The point is: I wasn't the president or CEO, or even a member of the senior executive team, but as vice president of organizational development I was able to significantly impact the direction of an organization and deliver results to the bottom line. Almost 20 years later, I still take pride in this story. You can deliver results from wherever you sit in your organization. It's how you think about it that's key. You can do it.

"It always seems impossible until it's done."

—Nelson Mandela

CHAPTER 4

Think Big. Start Small. Move Fast.

Whether you've arrived, or are on your way, it's not enough to develop the skills I'm sharing in this book and then stop. To keep your edge, you've got to hone those skills every day. Thus, the fourth principle. Think of your career like a basketball game. It is fast moving with lots of parts. Trust me, your competition isn't kicking back with their feet up on a desk and relaxing—at least not for long. Principle four is your breakaway move.

Among other things, to keep your edge you've got to:

- Stay on top of your industry
- Network like crazy
- Stay on top of your competition
- Stay educated about as many new technologies and practices as possible

- Stay healthy
- Stay focused on your goals
- Stay agile
- Stay prepared
- Stay flexible
- Create a strong brand
- Learn to filter and make decisions on the fly
- Think outside the lines
- Learn to lead by becoming influential and a people person
- Learn how to use your influence for good
- Develop leadership skills that last, that are sustainable
- Learn to deal with temptation
- Keep a number of chess boards (options) in play at all times
- Learn to lead, and lead well

Leadership is a multi-faceted ability, and something most of us equate with power. True leadership, the kind that gets you remembered, and buildings and streets named after you, is all about influence, not power. Influence is the ability to get people to trust you, listen to you, and act on your behalf and according to your work, moral, and ethical standards. Dr. Martin Luther King Jr. was powerful, but not because he was good at giving orders and demanding things of those around him. He was powerful and feared by those who opposed him because he was an influencer. You don't become an influencer, or a leader, overnight.

Leadership is a marathon, not a sprint. Leadership is something you do with people, and not to people. That's where the concept of sustainable leadership comes into play. How do you begin your journey and grow into a big impact, long-term leader that people look up to and value? How do you incorporate your technical expertise and your leadership abilities in a way that allows you to build a long-term, sustainable, high-impact career? That's what we're talking about here.

This is where being clear about your health, your values, your finances, and investing in your network is crucial. Remember, when you are playing multiple chess boards at the same time, you don't have to worry about someone confronting you with ultimatums or with values that don't fit with yours. They no longer have control over you simply because you work for them. You don't have to lose everything because someone is handing you options that don't fit your values or what you or your brand represents. Have a value set that's really clear, so that when you're presented with something that doesn't fit that set, you're in a position to say, "No, I don't believe in that. I believe in this." Those are the keys to building a long-term, sustainable career model.

Leadership and sustainability

A lot of people talk about certain skills–listening, talking, following-up, and following through–but few people talk about compassion, boundaries, ethics, work ethic, morals, or personal religious faith. A great leader grows stronger over time as their wisdom increases and as respect for them gets stronger. This is how leaders become influential. People see them, experience their actions and decisions over time, and learn to trust them. When you trust someone, they can influence you in a way that no one can buy. They earn a place inside your head and your heart. They become part of your inner circle and what they say has weight. You're willing to listen and act on what they say because you have seen they act with honor, integrity, and with your best interests at heart.

Leadership is really about what people will do on your behalf when you're not in the room. Are you a good leader of a family? When you're not there with your kids, how will they show up? What will they do? Do they remember the messages that you put inside of them? When you're not with your group or your team–do they still act as if you were? Do they model the values that have been modeled by the leadership?

It's a living legacy: the things that you stand for, the things that you push for, the things you believe in, the energy you create influences others in powerful ways. Are you able to extend that into and through others so that they engage and behave in a similar way to your values and goals? When people see that, they can recognize that they are connected to you, respected and influenced by you.

In earlier chapters I've referenced people who have worked for me, some of them multiple times, and even though they don't all work for me now, I still consider them part of my team. Even though they're at other companies, they have a sort of "Orlando thumbprint" on them. Others may recognize that, and hopefully that thumbprint is a good thumbprint. That kind of influence is really about creating a leadership reputation that is big and powerful. It extends beyond just the people who you're communicating with at a given time. It's something that lives on and outside of you. Think of it like a ripple of leadership impact–it's your reputation.

Management is easy to see if I'm standing in front of a room of people who are working with or for me, and when I ask them to do something and they go do it. Leadership is about creating the kind of relationship where, even if I'm not there, they know what we need to do and the way we'd want to do it, and it still happens and gets done. That's your reputation. That's your influence. That's what allows a person to be a great and impactful leader, and that's what allows a person to be sustainable. Sustainability is when what you've asked to be done continues to be done, whether you're still part of that organization or have moved on. It's about having an impact that allows the things that you believe in, or the practices that you institute, to have a life that extends beyond the time you are there.

The skills to last

There are a few fundamental skills that are no-brainers for this. Communication and relating to people is foundational to your ability to build a team or a community, to relate, to enable things to happen, and be a decent human being. It's everything. That's a key element, as is being agile in your thinking, style, and approach. I don't think leadership is a recipe in the sense that it's something that has an exact plan to follow. You have to assess your situation, you have to assess the people that you're dealing with, you have to assess the environment you're existing in–and then, based upon those inputs, figure out the best approach or style to engage for that moment.

There are some more obvious skills in this category, too. Being empathetic, for instance, instead of yelling or standing on the table, will always win you more followers. Being quietly humble and confident is another way you project a sense of leadership, of being in control, centered, and focused. But there are contradictory approaches: knowing when to push people, knowing when to give a person space, knowing when to give detailed directions or trust someone's intuition, or knowing when to give someone a verbal kick in the pants. All those skills are also required to be an effective and impactful leader but knowing when to use them is really the trick.

There are a slew of leadership classes, books, or sabbaticals offered these days. There are definitely lessons to be learned in those seminars and situations, but on the whole, the thought of "I'm going to be a better leader, so I'm going to take a class on it," is not one that crosses my mind all that often. Instead, I think of leadership as a practice, like writing, painting, yoga, weightlifting, meditating, whatever you do every day with concentration. Every day, I take mental notes about those I work with and those I work for, and how they handled situations. Whether it's from those better, more impactful leaders, or from those who handle things in ways that I wouldn't, I learn to either emulate them or I learn from their mistakes. It's sort of like collecting acorns. I'm always collecting little tidbits of insight, information, knowledge, and skills that will make me a better manager, leader, business executive, and human. I test, and try, and pick up the things that I think will work and make me better. It's a lifelong practice, not one you can learn in a weekend or a month of slideshows and breakout groups with like-minded, would-be leaders.

Set up your chess boards

"Setback" is not really a word that I use. I think everything contributes to making you better, or making you different, even "setbacks." This is another return to the concept of playing multiple chess boards at the same time. Even a "setback" might be a really strong power move on one of your other chess boards, if you've thought about those things. Every time I try to take a career move, I try to think, "How does this play out on all three chess boards?" For example, before Holland America Line, I was the head of HR for Marsh & McLennan Companies–an excellent job. My boss saw something in me and decided to challenge me with some new areas. From that platform, I was given more responsibilities, and I took on marketing, communications, and corporate social responsibility.

Then I was presented with the opportunity to move into the business and lead and manage a P&L–a profit & loss statement. I had never formally managed a P&L before, and this was a large one. I was fortunate in the fact that my first P&L experience was $600 million. That usually doesn't happen. Usually you get $10, $20, or $50 million as your first P&L experience. To get a $600 million P&L out of the gate is unique–a great opportunity, but also a great risk.

I thought about it across all three chess boards. What's the worst-case scenario? I go, I do it, I decide I hate being a P&L leader, and then I migrate back into HR. But, even if I migrate back into HR, I'd be a better HR executive for having had the experience of managing a P&L for a couple of years. Or, I love it and I do really well there, and I continue to expand in growth and responsibilities right here inside of Mercer. Great. That's a good scenario; that's another chess board. Or else: I get this experience, and decide I want to leverage it, but that I want to take it in some other directions. Run a business in another industry, or get into private equity, or do something completely different. But those opportunities are afforded to me because I took the first risk. Whether it works out perfectly or not, it can still propel you in your career because it might open a different door.

I think the term "setback" comes in when you think about

your career as a straight line. You might think, "I'm going to go from here to there, and if I hit a bump or I have to go 'back,' then that's a setback." Instead of setbacks, I think a career morphs, and goes left, right, up, down, and around. What some call a setback I would just call a turn or an evolution of your career. An opportunity to reset. It's all in how you look at it. When you look at things in only one way, you're bound to miss opportunities that come about because you're in a direction that might have been considered off the original course.

> I believe that life and death exist in the tongue.

Your attitude, your approach, the language that you use as you speak about things, those are quite powerful, particularly in the concept of leadership because others take their cues from you. Even when something "bad" happens, a good leader responds to the bad with this kind of perspective: "Hey, guys, we're good. We're in good shape. Here's how we're going to get through this. We'll navigate through this situation; I'm not too worried..." or, "We were going to go right. Now we just need to go left, and then we can get back..." That positive, can-do, we've-got-this-covered attitude is absolutely critical to conveying the right message. You're telling yourself first, and then conveying the right message to others around you, so that you create the right energy. I've always maintained a positive attitude around just about anything I've dealt with. I've always been able to maintain time to crack a joke, laugh, or smile, even in the midst of something quite challenging or difficult, because that's just what I believe in. It has served me personally, and it has served me professionally in being able to influence others.

Making the next move

So, how do you manage all of these elements of your leadership? Multiple chess boards, adapting your approach to different scenarios, knowing what moves to make, keeping your connections open... it's a lot to juggle at once. Clearly you want to stay open so as to have as much opportunity as possible, but you also have to develop the skill or ability to filter facts and circumstances quickly, to make a definite decision, and then move on. Some people get caught in different phases of these situations. They may be awesome networkers. They network and network and network. They know everything, and everybody, but they never ultimately filter out everything competing for their attention and chose a path. Being super-networked without translating that into some plan of action or point of decision is not really good.

You have lots of opportunity, but you have to ultimately filter. You have to make some decisions: "I think I want to do this, and based on that, I'm going to make this move." Now, you have to look at the worst-case scenario, the best-case scenario, other alternatives or options that could play off of that move. If you can manage the worst-case scenario, and you're excited about the one or two options that could get created by that move, then that sounds like a good move to make. Once you make your decision, execute it. Don't spend a lot of time wishing for or missing what you thought you missed out on. Don't look back or waffle about your decision.

I've come to a lot of different forks in the road in my career. When you get to any fork in the road, know what phase you're in. When I'm at that fork in the road, I'm trying to decide. I tap into all those sources that I talked about, my personal Board of Directors, my network, and my own history. I reflect on the different pros and cons of the moves on these various chess boards, and I spend some good hard time thinking, "Well, how does this play out?" Then once I decide, I say, boom, "I've decided. Now I'm going to move forward." Once I move forward, I execute. I don't second-guess my decision. I don't hem and haw and say to myself, "Man, I wonder if I should have taken this job. Maybe I shouldn't have..." I can't do that. Even if I thought I should have, I can't afford to hit pause and think about it, because by then it's too late.

I have to execute in the job that I have. While I'm executing, I maintain a little bit of room for networking. Some people are really good executors, but they execute to the detriment of their network. They might get into execution mode and ignore their network for five years, then something happens, and they need it–well, it's gone! They haven't fed it for five years. Networks are a system that requires energy on all ends. Making your move is about assessing all the different chess moves, filtering, making a decision, executing, and then as you execute and get comfortable with your execution, you then have to lift your head up and reinvest in your network for the next go-around, whenever that might be.

How do you develop those filtering skills? You practice. Filtering is about making good decisions quickly. To make any decision quickly and well, you need to have experience making bad decisions and wrong decisions. You need to be a calculated risk taker. You have to learn to be open to making decisions based on your gut instinct or intuition. All those skills come from making any decision and debriefing yourself on the outcome. Parenting is a great way to learn to filter and to make decisions quickly. So are sports. Anything that requires making a choice on your feet, without all the facts, without weighing every possible outcome, but looking at the most likely outcomes, is a great way to learn to filter.

Again, I've discovered the secret to filtering and making those decisions while on the fly is to know as much as you're able to discern, and then determine what the worst possible scenario is. If you can handle the worst outcome, there's no decision or risk you can take that will destroy you. Having that freedom to choose without over-sweating the consequence gives you power and a clear head to do what you need to do.

Agility training

What about the leader who ends up taking on too much? It's a challenge. People talk about a work-life balance. I don't think you ever really get a set balance. It's like riding a bicycle. You're constantly making adjustments, shifting left, shifting right, braking, speeding up, and doing whatever you need to do to stay upright and move forward confidently.

Finding that perfect balance and developing the agility to move from your personal life to your professional life means recognizing what your priorities are. It means prioritizing your values and being committed to not getting pulled, or sucked, into chasing things outside of your priorities, no matter how enticing they may be. Think of your life as a suitcase. You can only pack so much into it before it overflows, or you break a zipper. Pack it too full and there's no room for anything new. Pack it with only one or two outfits and you're going to be ill prepared for whatever comes along. Over time you learn how much you can pack into your life (suitcase) and what's important and what's optional. You learn to balance your bag, so you travel well and enjoy the journey.

There are varying degrees of imbalance. If you're constantly chasing down the sweet spot and you're focused more on the potential fall than the forward momentum you're making, work and life are not going to be fun or flow smoothly. There are times when I'm really overcommitted to work and trying to manage things inside my direct job, and then I'm ignoring something else–my family or my network. And, like my family, I consider my network a part of my universe that I have to feed. I have to do my job, I have to engage with my family, and I have to manage and stay connected to my network. It's inevitable that you get out of balance, but when you do, you learn to pick yourself up and get back on track.

Depending on where you are in the cycle, you may pick stuff up. For example, I've always tried to invest in vacation time with my family. We've been to South Africa, Asia, and Australia–all over the world–where we have been able to spend significant time as a family unit. Not only is this an investment in my family, it's an investment in my mental health. If I take on a new job, for the first several months I'm going to be over-focused there. I have several charities that I try to support–probably too many. I have to manage that, because my philanthropic efforts around education and access are important to me as well.

So, I spend a lot of time really fighting imbalance. People who are truly successful like to get stuff done. In my experience, successful people like to have an impact. If I have idle time, I create new challenges for myself. Six years ago, I hadn't written any book. Now I've written two. Before I started, people challenged me about it. They asked, "Why haven't you written a book, Orlando? You should really write a book," but I wasn't ready.

Then, I made a decision to make myself ready. First, I committed to it, and then I figured out how to do it–and then we got it done. A number of people have said, "Gee, Orlando–I don't know how you do all of this!" To that I respond, "Well, in the time it took you to write me that note wondering how I did it, you could have made a decision and started the process yourself."

Going strong mentally like that requires that I'm in touch with my own energy. Sometimes I have to force mind over matter, but it's really important to me to read my body, check in, and take time for myself as well. There are some days where I've been really running hard, and I can tell I'm getting tired, so I will take some time for myself, to refuel. That could mean I decide to push my morning meetings and sleep in a bit, or it could mean going golfing or watching a crime show on TV. It could mean leaving work early and going out to my son's school—watching my sons play sports is one of my favorite things to do. When their games are going on, I'm thinking about nothing else but watching them play.

I didn't start out that way. Early on in my career I didn't take the time. I abused myself pretty badly and I found out quickly that it wasn't sustainable for anyone. Over the years, I've had to learn to read myself and know when I need to take some time. Most CEOs and senior executives will present themselves as if they're superhuman, going all the time. They'll say things like, "I'm up at five, and I go jogging for ten miles first. Then, I have a latte and come into the office." We don't always talk about it openly, but we are human beings, and we all take our time in our own ways. I've learned it's important to protect my mental and physical health because I don't want to be that executive who works their whole life only to finally retire, get sick, and then die. I've seen that happen to people.

I very seldom talk to people who say, "I recognize I'm getting tired." Over time, there will be a cumulative effect if you don't start doing this internal assessment and try to get a little more balance. You're never going to be fully balanced. Who is? But you can strive toward some balance that works for you in that moment.

Exhaustion sneaks up on you, and each year as you get a little older your model has to adjust. I had a manager who had torn the ligaments in his shoulders from years of carrying those big garment bags. When the roller bags came out and they had the lighter bags, he was like, "Ah, I don't need that; I've been using these duffel bags for years." Well, years of dragging that duffel bag literally shredded the ligaments in his shoulders. There, two things happened: technology advanced (there were much lighter bags with wheels on them and he could have embraced technology), and his body was getting older. He missed out on both counts.

As we think about our career, it's the same thing. You're getting older, you're getting smarter, and you're leveraging people. That's when this whole idea of leadership comes into play. Where are the areas you can have the biggest impact? What will make you unique and special? Go and deliver that and let other smart people do the rest.

Trade-offs

This career journey is about trade-offs. You'll have to maintain the imbalance between work and life, and you'll have to manage playing multiple chess boards. Getting ahead and creating career momentum is a lot to sign up for, and as I've mentioned there will be moments where you will have to make a choice. I'll give you a personal example.

When my son was 10 years old, he told me he wanted to play basketball in college. He's not an NBA prospect or anything like that. He's a smart and engaging young man who simply loves basketball and wanted that to be part of his college experience. His mother and I committed to him that we'd do everything in our power to make that dream a reality for him as long as he maintained the academic side of the equation and he put in the work.

So began several years of driving to AAU tournaments, sitting in gyms and cars with sweaty prepubescent boys, but my son achieved his outcome. He was accepted at a wonderful D3 college and was recruited as a member of their basketball team. As you can imagine I was proud of and excited for my son, and I had also promised him when he was 10 that I'd be there for his first game.

Fast-forward to his freshman year. At the time I was a senior executive and a key part of the senior leadership team, and it turned out that my company was planning a leadership retreat for a cross-section of the top 300 leaders from across the company on the same weekend as my son's first career basketball game. The meeting was an important meeting to shape the culture, strategy, and future of the company and I'll be honest, I had a little stress about this given the importance of the meeting. But I had absolute clarity of what to do. I needed to be at that game. My son is going to be my son way longer than I was going to be an executive at that company, and, honestly, if people didn't understand this desire to support my child, then maybe it wasn't where I should be.

Of course, I can say this now and make it sound way easier than it was. I was pressured by my bosses who said I "needed to be at the meeting."

The pressure made me think. What would happen to me if I went to the basketball game? Would I lose my job? Probably not, but I might lose my support and momentum. What if I didn't go to the basketball game? The promise I made eight years prior would be broken and we'd miss a wonderful story to revisit and celebrate for the rest of our lives. So, my answer was clear. I went to the game.

As you pursue career success, each of you will have to make similar choices, some small and some large. You will have to decide what works for you and your family. My suggestion is that yes you will have to trade-off on some of the smaller things. You may not make every parent-teacher conference, family dinner, or practice–or even games. But you want to do all you can to make the BIG things. Again, it's not a perfect balance, but in my household, for the most part, it was an understandable balance that worked. And I'm so glad I was at that game.

Temptations

Like I mentioned earlier, there have been a couple of different instances where I've been presented with the opportunity to be "let in." If I were willing to bend the rules a bit, I would be let into the kingdom, sat with the Knights of the Round Table, and "all secrets would be revealed."

I advise strongly against this. First of all, that's not a sustainable model. If you're going to lie, steal, and cheat a little bit, then somebody else is going to lie, steal, and cheat a little bit on you, and suddenly you're living in an episode of "The Sopranos," where somebody's trying to whack you, and you're trying to whack them. I choose not to manage my career with that kind of risk and stress. It's an important distinction, because some people will try to manage their career by hitching their wagon to someone's in front of them who promises to take them to new heights. The spoken or unspoken deal is that as long as you execute things on their behalf–whether they're right or wrong–they'll take care of you.

That's an approach, but it's mostly likely not a sustainable approach. It's definitely not sustainable on multiple chess boards. If it works at all, it only works on one chess board. If your whole career strategy is about making sure a particular person is doing well, he or she is only playing one chess board and you're limiting your opportunity. If you're building a brand and a reputation that's market- or industry-wide, then you can apply your skills to other chess games if you need. It gives you more options. I've always believed in trying to maintain independence. I was always aligned toward my bosses and worked hard to support them, but I also made sure I protected and developed my own network, so I could maintain opportunities in other industries as well.

You just say what's right or wrong relative to what you believe, and then you move accordingly. If you aren't strong in personal, financial, and career health, it does make it difficult, because you may be distracted with concerns like, "Gee, if I leave this job, or if I go do something else, what'll happen..." The domino effect starts, and then you find yourself doing things that you wouldn't do, but you feel like you have no choice. Avoid being trapped. Lead your life, instead of letting it lead you along.

Work is important—but it's just work. Go back a job or two, or even a month or two. Think about that really important job or that really important project. In the moment, it was the most important thing you needed to do. You worked really late, and you took your stuff home. Where's that stuff now? Where are those people now? Chances are, they're gone. I can think back 10, 12, 15, 20 major initiatives, and at that moment, I needed to do whatever had to be done. I needed to stay up all night to do it. And I did it, right? That's what was required to get the job done. Now, looking back, it was work. It was a project. We did what we needed to do, and we got through it.

But what is sustainable over time is the way I treated the people, the way I delivered, the relationships I made, and the impression that I left. Good, bad, or indifferent, that's what's still living today.

Go back and list one or two projects. Of course, hindsight is 20/20 and we have a clearer vision of the facts once it's in the past. That project wasn't as important as you thought it was. How you *handled* it was what was important. Go in with the knowledge that you've been there before. This project, too, shall pass, but your reputation will linger.

At the end of the day, it's work! What's the worst-case scenario? The worst-case scenario is somebody says, "This isn't good work. You need to go work someplace else." That's my worst-case scenario. And, 99 percent of the time, my work has been good enough. In fact, most of the time, it's been better than good enough. You have to deliver and execute–I don't ever want to suggest that you don't deliver and execute. However, you have to pay attention to the bigger picture of what's important in the long run. It's a unit, and you've got to do all those things to manage your career.

If it happens to you, don't think you're the only one being tempted. You're not. And being tempted isn't wrong, it's par for the course. But it's succumbing to temptations that often brings the greatest leaders down. Temptations run the gamut–financial, sexual, emotional or others. They can be big temptations flying red flags and banners that shout, "Wrong! Run away!" Or, they can just be doing an illegal or questionable favor for a friend or someone you don't want to disappoint. It's the small temptations that grow into big temptations.

Don't think "just this once," or "he's my friend and he'd

do it for me" to justify doing something wrong. When you give into temptation, you plant a seed in your character–a seed that grows. You tell yourself, "nothing happened last time, so it's not a big deal." The thing is, all actions, good or bad, have consequences. Your decision to cross the line will come back to bite you. And, while you're waiting for it to do just that, you're looking over your shoulder wondering when it will happen. That's no way to live.

Everyone talks about the benefits that can come from being a leader, but few talk about the struggles that come with power–including the temptation to do something you might never have done earlier in your career.

The room at the top

Many people who make it to the C-suite become arrogant, take others for granted, or feel justified in stealing, hurting, ignoring, or using others. They may become cynical, feeling like all people want is money, favor, or other resources from them. The room at the top isn't all rainbows, freedoms, and unlimited finances. It involves new struggles, new challenges, and harder choices. Things aren't always as clear as they seemed to be when you were a mailroom clerk or a new salesperson. Sometimes people want, even demand, that you compromise your values or beliefs if you want to stay at the top.

I suggest people be true to themselves, even when it means sacrificing a job, a career, or an opportunity. In the short term, it might hurt to stand by your values, but at the end of your career I guarantee you can look back and be proud you did. Making a decision to give into temptation is tough. It takes a lot of thought, a lot of weighing and examining your values and what you represent. It's a reality that you are going to have to choose. Not everyone is at the top because they are a prince or princess among thieves. Many times, those at the top are actually the thieves.

Only you can decide if you want to be the kind of man or woman who fears no one's accusations, or if you want to be the kind of man or woman who's always looking over their shoulder and collecting enemies who can easily use your weakness to bring you down. Don't think for a moment that you're the only one who knows you've given into temptation. Lots of people, the ones who make the critical decisions about your career, know.

Choose wisely. If in doubt, don't do it. If you've heard the Bible story about Adam and Eve and the serpent, you know that the forbidden apple probably looked and tasted amazing to Eve, even though she had been warned about eating it. That's how temptations are. They look small and inconsequential. Eve's one small bite had quite the repercussions. Like Eve, you have no way of knowing how giving into just one small temptation can potentially impact you.

Moving on

When it's time to move on to a new company, having a strong network and multiple chess boards in play will help. Now, it is important to note that playing on multiple chess boards doesn't mean you're being disloyal to your current employer. It doesn't mean you're not fully committed. Companies may try to put that on you, saying, "Oh, you're not really all in. You need to be all in with your job." But you can be absolutely committed to your job, delivering, executing, getting stuff done, while also not being an indentured servant that owes everything about their being to the corporation. You owe something to yourself, your skill set, your craft, and whatever your expertise is and honing that. Then, you need to figure out what the best exchange is between you and a corporation at any given time.

There is nothing wrong with that. To say that you're not committed when you're working like that is incorrect. It's very important to know this, because the corporation may put that language out there to try to make you feel bad for having another thought, which then ties you to the job. I actually think it makes you a worse employee. Because if you're indebted to the job and you're terrified about losing it, then what do you lose? You lose your edge. You lose your ability to be honest, to be courageous, and to push new ideas and innovate. Your whole goal is just to keep your job. That's a lose-lose for the company and for the individual. The individual is miserable. They're ashamed. They're mad. They're frustrated. They're a shell of themselves, and the corporation is not getting anything more than just a passive executor of some mundane tasks.

The bottom line here is that you need to know when to walk away and not look back. Learning to let go in order to go forward is hard but much easier than staying. You can't soar if you are weighed down by regret, anger, or any kind of longing for the past. Look forward and know that your path is not about what you did *before* but what you can do *next*. I know it won't be easy. It never is for anyone, really. But, the power of time to ease any regrets you may have is, as they say, on your side.

In the next section I'll share with you my take on one of the most important ingredients in your career–creating a global curiosity. Today, if you are going to take the path to accelerate your career, you must include global curiosity, interest, and experience as key elements in your success.

Truth and the value of real conversations

One of the things I always say when I'm talking to young people, one of pieces of advice I give consistently, is that they need to become comfortable with going global. As Thomas Friedman of *The New York Times* said in his 2005 best-seller, "The World is Flat." As I have shared, the three years I lived in Turkey gave me the most personal and professional development I had anywhere.

One of my favorite stories changed my perspective on how I communicate. In the U.S. I've noticed we have a way of talking that is very safe. Think about the times you have been at cocktail parties talking about weather, sports, or other topics of small talk. We all know the cardinal rule of conversation in mixed company--avoid topics of race, religion, and politics.

But something changed for me when I moved to Istanbul with my family. Soon after arriving, my wife and I hosted a dinner party with some of our new Turkish friends.

Now, Turkey is 98 percent Muslim and we happen to be a Christian family, and we wanted to make sure we avoided any potentially controversial topics. We had prepared and practiced for all types of safe conversations that we thought would relate to the community we were in, such as the local soccer teams: Besitash, Galatasaray, and Fenerbache.

So, the party started, and at the dinner table, over appetizers, one of my new Turkish friends turns to me and says, "Now, Orlando, tell me about this man Jesus that you guys love so much."

You can imagine our surprise. My wife was kicking me under the table, and she whispered, "Well, what do we do?"

To which I replied, "You can't deny Jesus, you should answer him."

We went on to have one of the most enlightening conversations I'd ever had, and it brought us closer together as friends, friends with whom we are still very close, even to this day.

A number of weeks after the party I asked my friend what drove him to ask the question about Jesus. His answer was this:

He said, "I wasn't trying to convert you, and you weren't trying to convert me, but it would have been insulting to come into your home and not talk about something that was not important to you. What did you want me to talk about, the weather?" To which I was thinking in my head, No. *Actually*, soccer.

To show us respect and trust meant to have an open and fearless discussion. My time in Turkey taught me to have real conversations with people, and it changed my perspective of the world.

I considered it an honor and an opportunity to have worked in the travel business, because I've seen how travel changes us and our experience of the world. Mark Twain once said in his book Innocents Abroad which was first published in 1869:

> "Travel is fatal to prejudice, bigotry, and narrow-mindedness, and many of our people need it sorely on these accounts."

Twain said it over 100 years ago, but it's still relevant to what we are experiencing in the U.S. today. Because in order to make real progress, I believe we need to challenge ourselves to cross perceived boundaries and talk about the things that are important to each other.

Since my time in Turkey, I now have real conversations with people. It has made me a better executive but also a better person. What one learns in an executive environment is that it is all about relationships and people. So, this experience has equipped me to be better at what I'm doing, and I'm better than I used to be at talking about issues of race, religion, and politics. It doesn't mean we always agree on these topics, but we can respect and understand one another's perspective, and that is the true definition of inclusion.

On December 1, 2014, I was named president of Holland America Line, a 140+ year-old cruise line. In the time before the COVID-19 pandemic, the company traveled to more than 400 ports, 120 countries, and all seven continents. We prided ourselves on delivering an "immersive destination experience" for our guests where people could touch, feel, and taste the local cultures, cuisines, and experiences. I personally believe we were changing the world in a small way through travel.

People have said to me, "How did you move from an HR globally-oriented career to leading a large cruise line? How did you get that job?" The most intriguing thing is that I took this job having never been on a cruise ship. I wasn't a customer or a fan of cruising before being asked to lead one of the more historic cruise lines in the world, so I give the Carnival leadership credit for progressive-talent thinking.

Cruising is a human-capital business and my expertise is in human capital. That's what was valued in this particular opportunity. Whether it was creating an environment to maximize the impact to employees, or creating a welcoming environment for guests who are travelers, at its core it's about people, and that's what I do.

Let me tell you a story to illustrate what I mean. When I worked for Coca-Cola, I served as the head of HR for Eurasia and Africa, based out of Istanbul. My leadership team was quite international, made up of Africans, Turks, Americans, Indians, Eastern Europeans, and Russians. In 2006, we planned our first leadership team meeting in Dubai, and as a part of the meeting we wanted to do some team building, so we went to the Ski Dubai indoor ski resort which is located inside of a mall.

The thing about Ski Dubai is that you could be standing outside in the middle of the summertime, desert heat, and within 15 minutes you could be bundled up in warm clothing, standing on an indoor winter ski slope.

We got started, and the Americans went first–swish, swish, swish–and they were down the slope. Great fun. Next came the Russians, and the same–swish, swish, swish–and they were at the bottom, cheering on the next group to take their turn.

The Africans stepped up to go next, and I watched in horror as they tumbled and slid their way down the slope. To this day I don't know how they got to the bottom without injury. When they finally reached the rest of the group watching, I asked, "I'm so glad you made it down OK. Haven't you skied before?"

Lots of shaking heads. I asked, "Why did you get up there and ski then?" They answered together, "You're the boss and you told us to ski, so we skied!"

I learned some important lessons that day. Most importantly, I learned to ask more questions of a diverse team of people, and to be more thoughtful about the cultural differences across the team. I loved my time in Turkey and across those 90 countries, and I learned so much about myself and other cultures and people. I know that the experience has served me well in the subsequent years, including in my time leading Holland America Line, taking guests all around the world.

This is also why travel can be so valuable, and I encourage you to get as much global perspective as you can. If you can get an ex-pat assignment, that is the best. There is nothing like experiencing the food, culture, and perspectives around the world. But if you can't get such an assignment, then challenge yourself to get as much global experience as you can in other ways.

When you travel, do you try to replicate the same experience as you get in the U.S. or do you venture out? Do you try to communicate and create relationships with people in those unique spots? This will give you a different context around the way you think. You want different perspectives to wash over you to help you expand your understanding and insights. And even if you don't get to travel globally, there is still opportunity to get global experience close to home. Try local restaurants that have different ethnic foods as another way to gain more global and diverse experiences within your own country. America is a mosaic of many cultures, and most major cities will celebrate many ethnicities in ways in which you can participate. Let these festivities inspire you to go visit those original countries when you have the opportunity.

Take a calculated risk

Try this mantra I use: *Think Big. Start Small. Move Fast.* Throughout this book I have asked you to think big thoughts for your career. To have something of some consequence, of some success, you have got to have a vision. It's that emotional element that will sustain you to keep you moving toward your vision. So, pull from things that are bigger than you. It may be, for example, a very memorable movie that holds a similar vision to the one you hold. Lean on those visions as your framework for success. Then, start small. This is a marathon, not a sprint. So, each job, each interaction, each experience is an element that goes into the creation of your career. Further ingredients you will throw into your career will develop as a collection of miracles and mistakes over the course of your life. Finally, start fast, so you can make that mixture, your unique career. These three steps make up the fourth principle. I have found, and I believe you will too, these simple yet profound tactics will make all the difference in your success.

"At the end of the day, people won't remember what you said or did, they will remember how you made them feel."

–Maya Angelou

CHAPTER 5
Be a Culture Builder: Storytelling

Successful businesses are often framed as being driven by great strategy, strong financials, or cutting edge technology, but my belief is that what makes a business great are its people. I know that sounds cliché, but it's true.

At the same time, it's more than simply amassing a collection of good, talented people in your organization. You have to bring them into an environment in which they can flourish. Otherwise you don't get the full benefit of the talent you've worked so hard to bring together on your team. The fifth principle, sharing stories, builds culture because stories help us make sense of the world. They inspire us to understand one another.

Culture is a word that's often thrown around as a catch all for everything that's "soft" or difficult to measure and quantify in a business. Yes, culture can be more difficult to measure, but it's the most important element of a successful organization. Management consultant, Peter Drucker, coined the phrase, "Culture eats strategy for lunch," and I believe this to be absolutely true. While this is an extremely important concept for enabling a successful business, many leaders avoid this because it's so difficult to measure and deliver in a tangible way. I think this creates a powerful opportunity to differentiate yourself as a leader. If you can be a culture builder within your organization, you can differentiate yourself as an extremely impactful and valuable asset, because here are truths about culture builders:

- They create an environment where team members can be their true authentic selves
- They create environments that promote collaboration and inspire innovation
- They attract talent
- They walk the talk by living the "rules" of the organization, assuming those rules are good ones

A culture is a collection of beliefs, behaviors, and assumptions amongst the people within an organization. You can't control what people believe or the assumptions they make, but you can align on an agreed-upon set of behaviors that we will work within together, under the umbrella of our company, organization, department, or team. The hope is if we work with an agreed set of behaviors, and those behaviors "work" for us, it will ultimately influence what we believe and the assumptions that we make.

Therefore, an important skill of a high impact leader is to be a culture builder. Do you build and live by a set of behaviors that promote employee engagement and collaboration? Do you create an environment where people can show up as their true full selves?

Are you a storyteller?

One of the most powerful ways to promote an agreed-upon set of behaviors is through storytelling. Stories celebrate employee wins, moments of going 'above and beyond,' collaboration between colleagues, or support of customers or suppliers. Telling powerful stories that illustrate the desired behaviors in your organization is a great way to help teach your team or organization how to engage.

In my own work life, I use various vehicles to tell stories, whether it's staff meetings, town halls, employee engagement videos, emails, blogs, or water cooler conversations. All are great ways to demonstrate the way you'd like things done within the organization.

For example, one day shortly after I'd joined Holland America Line, I was riding the elevator, and the doors opened.

Two employees were standing there, looking back at me like a deer in the headlights. One of them said under her breath, "It's him!" and they let the doors close again without getting on.

Now, do I seem like a scary guy?

But there was a built-in belief that there was a divide between senior leadership and the rest of employees. This had created a culture where people were afraid to share ideas with their leaders, hindering innovation. How in the world would we be able to do all the things we needed to do to reinvent our business if employees were afraid to get on the elevator with me?

So, I set out to make that one of the first things we began to change. Soon after that experience, we had a Town Hall and I told the elevator story. I made it clear to all employees that not only did I hope they would ride the elevator with me, I also wanted to hear what they had to say if something was on their mind, because it was the only way we are going to get better and do things we'd never done before.

Because here's the thing: there is a direct connection between an environment of communication and trust with employees, how the business is perceived by your customers, and how it performs. Employees have to feel like there is an open channel of communication for bringing the ideas they might be holding under their desks to the top for consideration. They have to feel safe and, in fact, be encouraged to fail fast.

Within a year, things were a little different when the elevator doors open. People got right on without hesitation and more often than not, we had a conversation about what was on their minds. I learned a lot about what our employees were thinking about and we drove a lot of change.

This is a simple example but is a powerful representation of what needed to change within the organization. If colleagues weren't comfortable riding on the elevator with me, they would never be comfortable sharing their ideas and innovations, and, more importantly, their problems and issues. We used this as a way to give people permission to open up with me, and each other.

In another example, we had an open house in the executive offices. Many employees had worked in the building for years and had never been in the executive offices, so we opened the doors and invited people in for refreshments and a chance to see the space. Employees took pictures at my desk and the simple experience of being in the executive office helped demystify the space.

Again, a simple gesture, but a story that employees told to each other and set the tone for the desired culture. I often ate lunch in the employee cafeteria and when I visited the ships, I would eat in the crew mess. We hosted innovation sessions where we encouraged employees to share their ideas and suggestions. We "celebrated" some of the better suggestions, and told those stories to the rest of the organization. All of these actions are intentional examples of the type of organization I wanted to promote, and each of these actions can become a "story" that employees shared with each other to understand the operating environment we were trying to create.

So, what happened? Within my first four years with the organization, employee engagement scores improved 8 points (that's a statistically significant improvement, and something that I am quite proud of), customer Net Promoter Scores also improved 7 points, we nearly doubled operating income, and we made significant improvements in ticket and onboard revenue.

Your authentic self

One of the lessons here is that it's very important that through it all, you are presenting your authentic self and being open to talking about tough topics. That starts by doing what you can to remove any fear you might be experiencing about having an open and honest dialog with people about some of our differences. We can't celebrate differences if we're afraid to talk about them.

> We must have the courage to have authentic conversations about diversity and a culture of inclusion or we won't have the kind of understanding and healing that is essential to lift us to a place where all people can be successful.

I know this isn't easy. For years, I managed my posture and the perception others might have of me--my car, my clothes, even my music. I'm from New Jersey, and I grew up in the rap era. Early on in my career, I would drive my car to work with my favorite music turned way up... maybe listening to something like Me, Myself, and I, by De La Soul. I'd play it until I got close to work, then I'd switch the radio over to something else and casually roll in listening to what I thought would be more acceptable to my colleagues. Maybe something like Move, by Miles Davis. I may or may not have been right about that then, I don't know. But what matters is that I wasn't showing up as my true self.

Another time, as the CHRO of Marsh & McLennan Companies, we were on an executive retreat and at dinner as a "get to know you" exercise, our boss asked each of us to go around the table and name our favorite movie. I was the only African American on the leadership team at the time, and as we went around the table it became very obvious that my favorite movie was very different than the others on the team. I decided to simply pick one of my colleagues' favorite movies and share it as my own. It was a quick decision, made without any thought, because I just didn't want to have to explain the context behind why it was my favorite movie.

I didn't think anything about it until the next day when we were having a diversity session and a discussion about how important it is for people to show up as their true, authentic selves. And that's when it dawned on me. If I, a senior leader at a company of more than 50,000 people, didn't feel safe enough to be my authentic self and share my favorite movie with my peers, how must people 2, 6, 10 levels below me in this organization feel when confronted with topics and issues that highlight race?

I stopped the meeting and admitted what had happened the day before, and we ended up having a real conversation about difference in a way that impacted how we talked to one another, and about authenticity in the company moving forward.

And by the way, in case you're wondering, my favorite movie is Glory.

So, I want to challenge you to be self-reflective and ask yourself what you are about? What do you really care about? And are you showing up that way at work? Also, in terms of an environment of inclusion, I have a good test for you to consider. Whom do you hang out with at work? Are you making an effort to go to coffee or lunch with people from different backgrounds?

And whom do you hang out with at home? When you have a dinner party, or you have friends over, does everyone around the table look like you?

Finally, what are you doing to create an environment where the people who work for you feel like they can show up authentically?

And if you aren't actively working to create such an environment, what are you going to do to change that?

Supporting a culture of inclusion and communication will require showing up authentically, having real conversations about the topics that matter most and sharing stories.

If you are going to be an impactful and powerful executive, you have to be intentional about the culture you intend to create. A great way to influence culture is to serve as the chief storyteller for your team or your organization. Being a great storyteller will help you be a great executive.

It all starts with you.

"Brand yourself for the career you want,
not the job you have."

–Dan Schawbel

CHAPTER 6
Build Your Personal Brand

A brand is anything–a logo, a name, a symbol, a design, an image, a food, a color, a sound, a musical note (think of the start-up sound of an Apple or Window's computer), a reputation, an emotion, a tone, a history, an employee–literally anything that separates one thing from another and conveys some feeling, awareness or reputation to the person viewing, hearing, seeing, or experiencing that brand.

You don't have to have someone tell you that a Mercedes, a Rolls-Royce, and a Rolex are expensive, high-quality status symbols that generally are a sign of wealth. You just know it because you've been exposed to their brands. When you see a logo for your favorite sports brand, restaurant, airline, or beverage, you might get a feeling, a hit, a rush of good feelings about it.

Why? Because their brand, which is the way you feel when you hear about them or see their logo, is one of quality, security, wealth, safety, and reassurance. Companies and corporations work hard to protect their brand because a brand is your reputation. It's what you stand for. It's what people expect from you when they interact with you or buy from you. When your brand is tarnished, your reputation and your business will be tarnished also.

Branding, in the context of a career, is your personal brand. It's just like branding in any of the products I mentioned--when you hear the name of a product there should be certain truths that come to mind about that brand. When you hear Mercedes, you think high-end, luxury, quality. We could go down the list of quality brand examples and their associations, but you get the point: brand = reputation.

In the sixth principle, the same issues are true when it comes to managing your career as it does for selling a product because you're always selling yourself. When you hold the door for someone, say "please" and "thank you," or show up well-dressed with shoes shined and a suit perfectly pressed and ready to roll, you're building your personal brand. Think of some of your friends. Now think of one who doesn't particularly care how he or she dresses or looks. Sometimes they're in sweatpants, sometimes they're in a suit. How do you think of them as a business professional compared with the guy who you never see unless he's in a suit and tie, polished and ready to go?

It's the same with you and the brand or image you project. People put you in a slot and think of you a certain way based on your actions, personality, dress, and who and what you are every day. Your brand is something you can work on enforcing and growing in a way that you can control, as much as possible, what people think of who you are. So, ask yourself, "What is my brand?"

When people know that they are going to work with you, or work for you, or be associated with you, what do you think comes to mind? When they find out, "Hey, you're going to get a chance to work with X," what is their response? "Wow, you're lucky." "He's great." "She's intense." "She's a good leader." "He's a good listener." "She's empathetic." "He's mean." "She doesn't listen." Or, "He's disorganized and lazy." What do people say about you?

Part of your ability to be successful is connected to what people say about you when you're not around. Their comments to others speak to the reputation that you have established. That's what people will pay for. That's what people look for. That's what they'll buy.

If you have a strong personal brand when you're job hunting, your brand tells your potential boss that you have a particular skill set or ability they want on their team. When you're working for a company and you know your personal brand as well as the company brand, you're in a position to get the attention of leaders who want what you can bring to the table. That's only possible if you are clearly branded. Think of it like this: if you walk into a store and see rows and rows of cleaning products, how do you know which one to pick?

It's up to you to learn how to maximize your potential, develop your brand, and break away from how others might initially perceive you.

I've lived in many diverse environments. In some settings I was perceived as acting "too white," while in other settings, I was perceived as "not acting black enough." During my youth, I was regularly challenged as an African American male growing up both in integrated schools and all white schools where my brother and I were the integration. Often, I found that people initially painted a picture of who I was based on their own history, which had nothing to do with who I truly was.

I learned that ultimately one has to develop a personal brand that is so uniquely yours that it shatters other peoples' biases without wasting time trying to prove anything to them. That's the goal.

Personal brand positions you to be remembered

Chances are you pick a product based on your familiarity with the brand, and how comfortable you feel with it, regardless of whether it is the absolute best brand or not. Now, if you're in a company where the top ten candidates are all equally qualified for a position, how do you think the supervisors or human resources determine who gets the job? It goes back to brand, or reputation. If you're known as the person who has other qualities (your brand) as well as the skill sets needed, then you're more likely to be selected simply because people recognize, trust, and like your personal brand.

One of the things companies have learned about brands is that when you dress up the same product you can charge more for it. For instance, soap manufacturers charge $1 for a basic bar of bath soap. If the company adds a fragrance, a pretty wrapper with a design, and maybe a ribbon on that same bar of soap, and calls it "Lavender Luxury," people will pay $5 for the same bar of soap. Why? Their perception of the soap has changed because the brand created an image of luxury in the consumer's mind.

That basic soap is now a branded luxury soap. Except for the fragrance, nothing much has changed about the soap itself. When generic products came on the market years ago people were sometimes pleasantly surprised that the product itself, in a black and white box with no branding, was as high quality as the expensive name brand. The truth is, they are often the same product. Only the packaging and branding is different. If your skill set is as good as everyone else's skill set, the best way to stand out is with a personal brand.

You can begin improving your branding and image simply by looking the part of the person you want to be. You'll need to change on the inside too, but branding can start with looking the part. From there, you need to decide who you want to be, who you are, and how you want to be perceived by others. Do you want to be known as the global traveler? The negotiation expert? The calm head when everyone else is losing theirs? Play to your strengths and develop those skills. They become part of your brand.

Your brand is critical because it will have a significant impact on your career. It's what sets you apart from everyone else in your company and your industry. A lot of the opportunities you can seize come and go before you even know about them. Whether they come or not, and how often they come along, has a lot to do with your brand and who is aware of it. To use myself as an example–I've had a chance to work for a number of companies over the course of my career. I've had a number of people work for me.

Some of those people worked for me several times, following me from company to company. I'd like to think that's a function of having a good brand as a leader and being a good person to work for. I've been afforded some pretty good opportunities in terms of people calling me and asking me about roles and jobs, or asking me to be on a board, council, or advisory Board. I think part of the reason why I get invited to many high-quality opportunities is because I have a good brand, reputation, and market that I've built up over 30 years.

But, at the end of the day, there are some basics. Before you can build a brand, you have to have some fundamentals. Do you deliver? Are you competent? Do you get things done? Do people like working with you? Assuming that those things are true–you're a good employee, you're competent, and people like working with you–there can be other things that you don't pay attention to that can have an absolute impact. For example, the way you treat people.

Some people are really good at managing up, or treating those higher on the corporate ladder well, and building good relationships with them. While they treat their superiors well, they treat their peers and subordinates horribly. News of that kind of different treatment travels from company to company and place to place. Some people don't pay attention to the details in managing up. While they may be very competent, do good work, and are loved by the troops, they don't have the support of senior management because they don't pay special attention to management. Sadly, one's career can stagnate because the executive hasn't paid attention to senior management.

Relationship-building, particularly as you get into more senior levels, becomes increasingly important. I'm not talking about false flattery or apple polishing. I'm talking about learning how to have honest, respectful, and professional relationships with those above, around, and beneath you.

Branding checklists

First, you need to know what your brand is. Otherwise, you can't query your brand regularly to see whether you're representing yourself as you'd like to be seen. Beyond that, you also need to know what you want your brand to be. When you say, "I want to be President of the United States," or "I want to be CEO of a company," whatever it is you want to do, ask yourself, "What's the brand of people that tend to get to those jobs?" There's a certain educational profile, a certain work history profile, and a certain kind of imagery that goes with those jobs. How you present yourself, your posture, how you dress–depending on how important it is to you, some of these things might require attention.

There are different checklists, such as the competence checklist. ("Did I have the right job experiences?" "Do I have good mentors and advocates to vouch for me?") Then there are other factors, such as your look and the way you dress. I've had conversations with people early on in their career wanting to get a job in corporate America, but they come out of college wearing the wrong kind of suit–a brightly colored suit, an ill-fitting suit, a cheap suit.

They might have the wrong hairstyle–the same haircut they got to fit in with their fraternity or to emulate their favorite rock band or rapper. In a perfect world, should those things matter? No. In a perfect world, you should be able to wear a purple suit. You should be able to have a 'fro or facial hair or dreads or blue highlights, or whatever your personal preference is. But the reality is that in today's society and business environment, there's a certain look that's expected, which is the look that gets recognized and rewarded in the corporate setting. Only you can decide which matters more to you–your personal style or your advancement through the rank and file to become senior leadership.

When I have this conversation I tell people, I'll never tell you what to do, and I'll never tell you to trade off what you believe in personally, but you do have to understand the implications. If you want to have dreadlocks, a nose ring, a tongue piercing, or tattoos up your neck, you're absolutely free to do that. This is a world where that freedom of choice exists. You have to understand, though, that there may be implications. People may not hire you, or they may have to look harder, past the external, to understand your quality and how good you are.

Think future-forward

Something that has helped me is to pay attention to people who were in roles that I was aspiring to in some way. When I was in college and people would come to speak–people that I was particularly impressed by, maybe told a story, or ran a company–I paid attention to them. I looked at them. And, again, there are the checklists, like what college they went to, what was their major, etc. But I also looked at things like their clothes, their suits, and how they wore the suits. It gets back to my story about the Blair Underwood character in LA Law. I had an image in my head based on that character and how he went to work, how he carried himself, and I thought he was cool. I tried to model some of those things--the briefcase, the car, the suit, or at least tried to position myself so that over time I could grow into that image.

One of the things I've always done, whenever I've taken on a new job, I've always updated my resume. So, when I take on a new job, one of the first things I do is crack open my resume, and then I rewrite the job description of my new job. This is, point for point, what I do. I start the gig, crack open the resume, and rewrite my future-forward. If I'm going to use this in two or five years from now, what are the things that I want to have accomplished? I try to write the paragraph in anticipation of what I intend to do, and then spend the next six months to a year and a half actually doing it. Then I go back and update it. Did I complete the things that I hoped to achieve? I think of it as prewriting the next chapter of my career.

This exercise makes it explicitly clear. Your career is a story that you're trying to tell. One of the places where you tell the story is in your resume. When you come into the role, what's that chapter going to say? What's that future chapter going to look like? I then try to execute it in the job and make it fit that chapter of my job and my life.

Earlier in my career, I aimed to realize those goals within six to twelve months. As I've become more senior, the challenges have become more complex, and the jobs have become bigger, I've adjusted my timeline to take somewhere between three to five years.

My close friends can tell when I start a new job and I'm in that initial period. When I jump into a new role, I usually disappear for six months as I'm figuring it out, meeting people, learning the culture, and paying attention to my environment and the way things are done at that job. As I get my arms around it, I resurface. My friends can tell, because suddenly I'm available to do things in the evening again. I can go golfing. I'm no longer a hermit crab. During that initial six-month period, I can't do any extra-curricular activities because I'm knee-deep in the new goal, whatever that new goal is.

What and how

You want to be able to draw a really clear line between the work you do and the impact it has on the company. The thicker and clearer that line, the better. That's why prewriting your job description from a resume perspective is useful. You want to say, "Here are the things I do. Here's my job," and describe the elements of the job. Then the next thing you want to do is say, "And here's the outcome that I have delivered," if it's past tense, or "that I will deliver," if it's future tense. Be really clear about what those outcomes are. Be able to say, "I increased revenues from this to this; reduced costs from this to this; delivered this, this, and this on time. Created this project. Hired this many people." Specifics matter because you can support those claims with facts and data.

All of this leads into the brand that you're trying to create. At the core of whatever it is you do, there should be a core reputation around delivery, getting things done, and having an impact. That's the what you should focus on. Hopefully you can do it in a way that's collaborative, celebratory, fun, energizing, enjoyable, and that makes you the perfect person to have around. That's the how.

There are lots of people who get stuff done, but they break all kinds of china and destroy lives and burn bridges as they do it. In my opinion, those people crash and burn. It's difficult to maintain sustainability with that kind of model. There are people who are wonderful to work for, but don't get anything done, and there are people who keep you around but never send you anywhere and make it difficult to have a career that advances into upper levels. I believe you have to master both sides. You need the *whats* and the *hows*.

Five steps to creating your own personal brand

- **STEP ONE: Create a vision of your personal brand.** This vision is simply the way you want others to see you, and how you personally want to live your professional and personal life. This process includes looking at your values and determining their priority in your life. Which is more important to you? Work? Faith? Family? Fun? Community? Knowing what your values are, and their priority, will help you make tough decisions when it comes time to choose between them.

- **STEP TWO: Prioritize your values.** If you're on your way to the C-suite, you will be challenged to choose between your values of family and work. You may work for a company that wants you to bend the rules to keep your job. What are your values? Knowing what they are and the priority you give them now will make it easier to stand by them later. When you know what your true values are, you know what your personal brand is too.

- **STEP THREE: Identify your passions.** Passions are things we love or are extremely interested in. Knowing what your passions are can help you determine where you want to be in five, ten, or twenty years. I was initially interested in engineering but discovered my passion was people and systems that helped people. Your passions and values help you get a big picture image of who you are, what you want to do with your life, and how you see your brand developing.

- **STEP FOUR: Identify your ideal character traits.** You can best do this through taking a series of personality tests online (most are free or low cost). What you're looking for is whether you're an introvert or an extrovert, whether you're conscientious and have a strong work ethic, or if you're more laid back and flexible. Do you make decisions with your head, your heart, or both? Are you agreeable? Neurotic? Do you have a strong emotional intelligence quotient (EI)? This means you have the ability to perceive, control, and evaluate your emotions, and the emotions of others, in social situations.

- **STEP FIVE: Talk about your values and traits with friends and family.** We've all got egos and blind spots that we can't see. However, family and friends are amazing when it comes to spotting our weak spots and pointing out our failings and shortcomings as well as our strengths. Go to them and ask for their input, impressions, and perceptions of you. Don't get angry or argue with them. Stay calm and ask for examples. For instance, if someone says, "You're always selfish." Ask them to describe a few times or instances where you have been selfish. Look for patterns. They may be right; they may be wrong. Asking for examples gives you hard facts to consider. Friends and family may be harsh or may be overly optimistic. Either way, they'll provide you with insights that you can't get by yourself.

Taking it to the next level

To take your career to the next level, and the next, means standing out and distinguishing yourself. Once you understand who you are, you'll be more equipped to find a way to distinguish yourself. One way that you can distinguish yourself is by taking on unique projects that might not be something that you would traditionally take on in your current role. You have to assess your risk tolerance. When you jump out and take on projects that others won't take, there are some risks associated with that. There's a reason why others haven't taken them. Think before you leap. Know what you're getting into and what the consequences and rewards could be.

If you can take on a risk and execute it well, it differentiates you and builds your brand. It shows that you're an innovator. It shows that you're one who will go above and beyond. Those are all good things that you want to have associated with your brand and the type of reputation that you want to have.

I would also encourage you to always think through thoroughly before committing. Ask yourself, what's the downside? What's the worst-case scenario? So long as you can own and manage the worst-case scenario, then it's a risk worth taking.

We talked earlier about my time in Turkey. I had been offered the choice to take an expat assignment in either London or Turkey and I chose Turkey intentionally because it was going to build a reputation for me. I intended it to be an experience set for me as an international business leader. While London would have been a great experience (I love London--it's a great city, glamorous, and historically important and central to the Western world), living in Istanbul and serving the Middle East, Eurasia, and Africa was an even stronger check in the "works internationally" column.

Turkey was a bigger stretch for me and my family. It was a big move and a much bigger culture shock than moving to London, where the hardest thing to adjust to is driving on the opposite side of the road. Choosing Turkey was absolutely the best thing I did, both personally and professionally, in terms of how much I grew personally, and what it meant for my career.

You need to push past questions of "How can I get by?" or even "How can I do well?" and pivot to "How can I do really great work?" Even if you grew up in the suburbs, never even visiting Canada, that's no reason to limit your brand by excluding the international angle. The best thing about your brand is that you create it. One of the things that I wanted as part of my brand was to be an international business leader. So, I started traveling internationally and then I started working internationally. Then, there was an opportunity afforded to me to live internationally.

I take great pride in the fact that I'm challenging my children to be international and insisting that they not only study languages but that they travel internationally. I've sent them to China for language immersion, and other experiences to broaden their worldviews because I want them to be even better than I am when it comes to their international exposure. I'm already thinking about the brand of my children based on what I've learned in trying to create my own brand.

When you think about it that way, your brand extends way beyond your work into who you are. One of the things my mother did for me when I was young was tell me I could be anything and do anything. A lot of mothers do this, I'm sure. But I really believed her! She got the brainwashing in good. She used to play Dr. Martin Luther King Jr.'s speeches for me when I was a young man, and just said, "Look, here's a great man, a great leader, and you have what he has. You can be great. You can do great things." That's something I grew up believing, and still believe.

From there, I picked up cues. I watched how hard my father worked. He worked for the government for 33 years, and I got a good example of the discipline it takes to attack corporate America. I also built up the confidence to do it my way. My father grew up in an era where you work for a company, put in your 30-plus years, work hard and deliver, get your gold watch, and then retire. I didn't take that approach. I tried to build a personal brand and reputation, a toolkit that had value—so whenever I joined an organization, there was some mutual value. I was going to deliver a value for the company, and they were going to deliver some value for me, and we would allow that to work. When we got to a point where it needed to be different, it could be different, and there's nothing wrong with that.

Since that approach is more in tune with where careers are going today, I think I was a little forward-thinking for the time. That's the attitude that I've always had. I've always joined a company 100 percent. I worked hard, tried to deliver based on what they asked and what I understood the challenge to be. I was creative inside of that, but I was also very clear on what it was I was looking to extract from the working relationship. I wanted to build my career plan for the long term and to create the win-win for both me and the company.

I think that's an important philosophy. A lot of people go into work thinking, "How do I make sure I take care of the company? And then I'll trust that the company will take care of me." For some people it works, and that's great. But it doesn't always work. The company changes, leaders change, strategies change, and then unfortunately, the people who think like that become the people that end up getting stuck.

The two skills that can keep you from getting stuck, no matter what position you hold or the approach you use, are networking and branding. Networking is simply the skill of building a large group of people who know what you can do and have to offer, and vice versa. Branding is developing a reputation for what you can do and have to offer.

I want to introduce you to three friends of mine to help you think about how to think about your own personal brand.

Brand Story #1: Billy Dexter

Billy is a partner with Heidrick & Struggles, the executive search firm. But Billy's personal brand is that of connector or master networker. He's innovative and creative. As an African American, I admire that he keeps an eye out on issues related to African Americans within the context of his work. And more than that, he is very open and giving, and always wants to be inclusive. He's one of the most selfless people I've ever met. He doubles his brand with his attention to race issues and inclusivity. He is always engaging and involving others, and he's a great guy. He is actually one of my favorite people.

Brand Story #2: Jenn Longnion

Jenn is a long-time colleague and friend. We both grew up as organizational development (OD) professionals. I initially hired her at Motorola and was fortunate enough to re-recruit her to join the team at Coca-Cola as well. She has developed a personal brand as being one of the best and most strategic OD, leadership, and culture change minds in business. She has leveraged her talent to become first the CHRO and then COO of Dollar Shave Club, Inc., and is now the founder of See & Free Consulting. I'm proud that someone as talented as Jenn has worked with me twice. Throughout our careers we've coached, counseled, and challenged each other whether we are at the same organization or not. She's a permanent and valued member of my personal board of directors.

Brand Story #3: Eric Hutcherson

Eric is chief people and inclusion officer at Universal Music Group. We also worked together for six years in a previous company. Eric's personal brand is that of master presenter. He is smart, charismatic, high-energy, collaborative, execution-oriented, and a leader. He can create a following of people like him, which is where the "charismatic" quality plays a part. People want to be connected to him.

These are three short examples with personal friends of mine. But the question to ask yourself is, what is your personal brand? How would your friends describe you?

Here is an exercise for you to try:

> For one week ask friends, colleagues, and others you know, to share with you the top three adjectives they would use to describe you. More often than not, you will hear adjectives that surprise you. Once you are aware, it will also help you to leverage your brand inside and outside of your workplace.

Up to the C-suite

In addition to knowing your brand, and expanding your brand, what you need to remember as you move up the ladder is that embracing the relationship piece is key. This is something I've had to manage—being explicit about your brand and brand values, and the brand and brand values of the company for which you work.

There needs to be utter clarity around that exchange because it's so important. For most, the company brand is bigger than the individual brand. However, in today's world, with social media and the like, it doesn't necessarily have to be. If I personalize it, I have a pretty good brand. When I join a company, I'm bringing my network, my brand, and my relationships to that company. There's added value in that. You want to make sure that the company gets your brand and appreciates and respects it.

I've been in situations where it's worked brilliantly, and they were very comfortable with it and leveraged it. I've also been in situations where it's created some negative energy—for example, when I'm getting requests for speaking engagements, or to be on boards, and my boss isn't. If that happens to you—is your boss okay with that? You want to make sure you're aware, so that you can manage it. You don't want to be surprised when there's some pushback or negative feedback.

Remember how I said before that relationship building is key when you're making your way up the floors? As you aspire to roles in the C-suite, you'll notice that people in senior positions for the most part are all very smart, they're very accomplished, and they've gotten things done. That playing field is pretty much level. As you get to the top of the pyramid, it becomes more about relationships than accomplishments. Do I like this person? Do I trust this person? Do I want to entrust the brand of this corporation in the hands of this individual? Do I want to fly around the world or sit in a board room with this individual? Do our families get along? Do we have similar interests? Those things start to come more into play, and so you have to pay attention to them. And, "pay attention to them" means being more open to those invites to join these people and start building those relationships.

I remember the first time I got invited to spend the weekend at a senior executive's summer home. My initial reaction was very negative. I took it as an intrusion. "I have my own family. Why do I want to spend my weekend with your family?" What I did not realize (and a mentor explained it to me) was that I was being introduced or groomed for more senior roles, and they were trying to create a higher level of intimacy.

This idea is particularly challenging for people who have historically been underrepresented–women and people of color–that may not be members of the same country clubs, or live in the same neighborhoods. In order to create that intimacy, a senior leader has to reach out and invite you into that world, and when that invitation comes, sometimes the person who's being invited perceives it differently and doesn't take it. I went through it and I've heard others comment along those lines:

"Well, gee... I don't golf" or "I'm not interested in going on the boat," or "I have a pool at my own house. Why would I want to come and swim in your pool?" However, those things are important if you want to be accepted and create that intimacy and connection that allows you to move forward and move up.

Ways to create a brand

There are many ways to create a brand. Begin by deciding who your target audience is. For whom do you want to work? Where do you want to work? Do you want to be a CEO or do you prefer the excitement of being a traveling executive? Do you envision yourself as a company man or woman? Or do you dream of being an entrepreneur? Once you know who your audience is–a corporation, a small company, or your own company–you can begin to focus on creating your brand. Further considerations include:

- Developing a reputation for excellence, helpfulness, consistency, and dependability works in any industry.

- Developing a visual or physical image of your brand (color, dress, logo, scent, sound, etc.). Do you drive a classic car? A new car? A motorcycle? Do you always appear impeccably groomed? Do you always wear a certain type or color of tie or jacket, or carry a leather briefcase? What do people associate you with?

- Figuring out who is your community. Are you active in social media? Which media? Twitter? LinkedIn? Facebook? Instagram? What do your posts say about your brand? Are you upbeat, positive, and helpful?

- Deciding whether or not to create a blog? Build your reputation as someone who is an expert in your industry by providing the kind of knowledge, information, and feedback others are seeking. If you don't blog, be sure to build your reputation and status on LinkedIn.

- Dress for success, whether you're considering a lifetime in the military, a corporate environment, or being the CEO and owner of your own company. How you dress sends a very loud and distinct message.

- Decide whether to create and/or associate yourself with an iconic event–either a conference, a workshop, or some event that clients, customers, and potential customers can attend to learn more about your company.

- Decide whether to make videos. Videos are the fastest growing, most powerful way to build your brand. Make videos that help people by providing information and answers to questions that your clients and customers have. Don't just make self-serving "We're an awesome company" videos. Provide value to those watching.

Finally, once you have started building your brand, you've got to protect it. There's a reason why companies drop the contracts of big-name stars who get involved in drugs, alcohol, or illegal activities. It's nothing personal. They're just protecting their brand. You have to protect yours as well. Set a Google Alert on your name and your company name, so any time someone posts something positive, negative, or neutral about you or your company, you are alerted and can decide whether to take action before it blows up and goes viral.

Check in frequently. Google your name and pay attention to what people are saying about you online. Many of the negative comments will come from "trolls" or people who just love to stir the pot. Ignore them and they go away. Don't get involved with them online, not even in private emails. They'll just post your email and escalate the situation.

Tweet your own messages but, of course, never tweet or post anything when you're tired, angry, frustrated, or sick. If you have an intern or someone else posting for you, as much as possible, approve all posts. We've all seen how just one inappropriate or bad post can bring down a golden reputation.

The goal is to protect the brand you've built or are building. Why is it important?

- 48% of recruiters and HR professionals refer to personal websites when deciding whether to hire you.
- 63% of recruiters check social media sites to find out more about potential employees.
- 8% of companies have fired someone for abusing social media.

You don't have to be squeaky clean, but you do have to be clean enough not to set off alarms in the human resource department, or give people pause before hiring you. That's why the sixth principle of building and protecting your personal brand is so important to accelerating your career.

"Every great achiever is inspired by a great mentor."

–Lailah Gifty Akita

CHAPTER 7

Build Your Career Community

Oprah Winfrey once had this to say about mentors:

"A mentor is someone who allows you to see the hope inside yourself. A mentor is someone who allows you to know that no matter how dark the night, in the morning, joy will come. A mentor is someone who allows you to see the higher part of yourself when sometimes it becomes hidden to your own view. I don't think anybody makes it in the world without some form of mentorship. And, we are all mentors to people, even when we don't know it."

Oprah Winfrey's fourth grade teacher was her first mentor. Mary Duncan, an elementary school teacher, saw something "special and different" in Oprah and she encouraged her–a six-year-old who was then shy and insecure–to read in front of the class. She mentored her in the basics, being comfortable with who she was.

Most successful and famous people have several people throughout their lives who inspire, teach, coach, and mentor them.

Even if you're not famous, someone, including your parents, has mentored you, taught you the ropes, helped you see the potential in yourself, or nurtured you in some way. Likewise, you've done the same for others–perhaps without realizing you've actually been practicing the seventh principle of building your career community

Mentoring is about sharing advice and counsel. I'm sharing advice, counsel, and wisdom on this particular subject of building a successful corporate career. I was fortunate enough to have two very smart parents who are students of the world and could always give me advice and counsel that is still helpful to this day. They're not out of touch. I've tried to repeat that in a similar fashion with my children. My children both study Mandarin because, from what I could see and my own career experiences, China is going to be an important part of our global economy. Ten or twelve years ago I began encouraging them to learn Mandarin and it's turned out to be a good bet. All of us as friends and parents have an accountability to take the things we are learning and see around us, develop that into some points of view, and then be willing to share that with people we care about.

My purpose for writing this book is to share these points

of view as part of my personal value proposition with a broader group. When we talk about success versus greatness, I hope that part of my legacy will include being helpful to others. That's the reason I do career counseling, and give speeches, and writing this book allows me to hopefully have a broader impact.

The most important qualities of a mentor

So, what makes a mentor? Obviously, there's some knowledge or information they have that a mentee would find helpful or useful. There's also a reason why they would be of help. They're either in a role that you want, or they have a skill set or a set of experiences that would benefit you.

Whatever it is, hopefully there's some transferable knowledge that would be of help to you. On the flipside, there's something or some reason they're likely to be inspired to help you. Maybe they like you, or like Oprah's mentor, they see something in you that inspires, fascinates, or speaks to them for some reason. They may be looking for a protégée. They may simply enjoy helping others. Whatever it is, the best mentors have a reason, logical or not, for deciding to invest in you. It's important you understand that reason because it makes a difference in the experience you'll both have.

In looking for my own mentors, I've searched for people who have a giving spirit. It's not always that way. Sometimes you can find someone who's willing to mentor you even though that's not their nature; you just have to work to pull stuff from them. I like to connect with or target people who naturally like to be helpful, and who like to give. Not only do they give more, they give more willingly and freely. It's a help and a benefit.

Finally, a mentor is someone who knows something that you don't know. Sometimes people end up in a "mentoring" relationship because they both like the same thing or have had similar experiences. There still is room for some help, but I find that if you have someone who knows more than you, or knows differently from you, you'll tend to learn and be stretched more.

Mentors don't have to know everything you're eager to learn. Many times we'll have several mentors at once, each one helping us in different areas. You may have a mentor who can show you how to do your job better. Another mentor may be showing you the way to manage your time more effectively. Yet another can show you how to shape and polish your brand. Mentorships can last a lifetime, or a few days, weeks, or months. It depends on your agreement, what you need mentoring in, and how quickly you learn. Mentors aren't meant to be parents, although some may remind you of a good parent. Mentors are coaches, teachers, and inspirational and experienced people who help you become a better person, a better businessman or businesswoman, and a more skilled employee.

Not everyone wants to mentor you

While it may sound like I drifted through life picking up mentors wherever and whenever I pleased, the truth is, not everyone wants to be your mentor. Think about it: You're asking someone who is very skilled, very much in demand, and very popular and pressed for time, to give up part of their life and schedule to make sure that you become a success. No one owes you mentoring. You earn it, in one way or another. The more in-demand, popular, and skilled someone is, the less likely you are to get their attention. How many people do you think Richard Branson mentors in a year? Probably nowhere as many as a popular teacher at your high school or college.

You can't just waltz up to someone successful and ask them to be your mentor, especially if you don't have a brand, name, or reputation. You've got to show them your value. You need to be able to effectively and professionally state your case and explain why it's to their benefit to mentor you. You can't come across as desperate, awkward, irritating or entitled. You've got to sell yourself. This is true even outside the C-suite. You're asking people to commit to helping you become a better person, a better employee, and sometimes even potential competition for their job someday. What do you have to offer in exchange?

Do your homework. What can you offer them in exchange for being mentored? If they were to get five requests for mentoring how would yours stand out? This could be something like a reference letter from a professor of yours who knows them and writes you a glowing recommendation. It could be that you have other skill sets they'd find valuable–such as being a great researcher, writer, IT person, or that you're just a very curious person. Whatever it is, you've got to find a way to show what you have to offer is valuable.

How to approach a potential mentor

Chances are that your dream mentor is someone else's dream mentor too. Approach them with a rambling, disjointed or effusive request of "Will you be my mentor?" and they're likely to say "Thanks, but no thanks." Approach them with a specific question, a solution, a good reason for your request and they're likely to say "Sure," or at least hear you out. Successful people like to help others, but they're particular about who they help because their time is often limited. They want to know they're investing in someone with real potential, not wasting their time with someone who is unfocused with no readily definable goals.

Have you read all their books (if they have any)? Have you listened to their talks, or read their research? Do you know specifically what they have to offer or teach? You're more likely to get a positive response to something like, "I read your book on X and combining Y systems to increase productivity. I'm an associate production manager in the widget department and I think if I understood what you're saying about Z systems better I could help my department increase production by 50%. Would you consider mentoring me for 30 days so I can learn more about Z systems?"

You've presented the potential mentor with a specific problem or issue where you want coaching. You've done your research, read their book about the issue and have a basic understanding of what they have to offer you. You've been very specific about what you want to learn and why you want to learn it. You've defined the period of time you think you'll need to learn this skill and you've respectfully requested they mentor you. I'd say your chances of a "yes" are pretty good.

Contrast that with someone who says, "You're awesome. I really like what you've done with the company. Would you mentor me?"

Who would you pick to mentor?

Mentoring is not necessarily friendship or giving advice

Just because someone gives you a piece of advice or makes some good suggestions, it doesn't mean they're mentoring you. That's more of a networking, colleague, or friend sort of thing. True mentorship involves responsibility–from the mentor to the mentee and vice-versa.

A good mentor is as committed to your success as you are. They take their role in your career seriously. Mentors add value to your career and your skill set. They don't just throw ideas at the wall and see what sticks. They are advisors. They're mentoring you (hopefully) because they can help you by providing solid advice based on their experience, connections, and insights. In return, your mentor expects to see you progress and take their help to heart. If you're not improving, moving forward, or learning, good mentors will think twice about the time they're investing in you. There are dozens of other people they could be helping, so make sure they see what they're doing for you is making you a better person, employee, entrepreneur, or mentee. Whether you realize it or not, you're accountable to them in terms of how you utilize what they're sharing.

Being mentored is not all about you and what you get from the relationship. You should be looking for ways to make your connection valuable for your mentor as well. Look for opportunities to introduce him to your network, resources, and other mentors in a way that benefits him/her. Not only does this give you the opportunity to practice the most valuable skillset you'll ever develop (giving), it lets your mentor know that their time and expertise are valued. If you're right out of college or feel like you don't have anything to offer your mentor, consider giving them a copy of a new book you've found helpful. Send them articles on topics you know interest them. Ask them if there is anything they would like to learn about that you could research for them. If you meet over coffee, lunch, or dinner, pay for the meal or drinks. Don't just take or make assumptions that they are there to cover your expenses as well as give you free insights and mentoring.

It used to be that mentorships were considered "short-term" and had beginnings and endings. Some still do, but where it's possible, make your mentorships endless. This doesn't mean you're forever meeting and learning, but the mentorship becomes a mutually beneficial relationship. It evolves into more than just you sitting at the feet of a master. It becomes two people who mentor each other in different areas, or who network, communicate, support, and help each other over the years. Some of my greatest friendships and members of my personal Board of Directors began with a good mentor.

Another important mentor quality for me is someone who's willing to be direct, honest, and even difficult or challenging at times. Knives aren't sharpened without friction. Likewise, people need some friction or challenge to improve as well. If you play sports, or you are a musician, dancer, or artist, you only learn by pitting yourself against better players, performers, or artists. Business is the same way. You learn more by going up against those who know more and do things better than you.

If a mentor has the knowledge, and knows more than you, their insights and coaching can be helpful. This is only so if you have to work for it. If they're too nice or sugar-coat their feedback, you don't grow as much. It's important to have someone who has confidence in giving direct, honest, and (sometimes) tough feedback, if that is what's required. A mentor isn't there to soothe your ego. They're there to teach, coach, challenge, and improve your performance, your knowledge and your skill sets. Don't think that because a mentor makes you angry or frustrated, or you feel inadequate around them, that they're a bad mentor. If what they're doing, saying, or showing you is making you better as a person, better at your job, and helping you improve, they're doing something right.

Success breeds success

I notice a lot of people like to give advice about things they know little or nothing about. As the old adage goes, "Don't take financial advice from poor people." It's true. There are books and movies about a random person with an empty bank account giving a young person advice that turns them into a millionaire or CEO. In real life, however, it rarely works that way.

The people you associate with as colleagues, friends, and mentors, define your brand and affect how people see you. Does the person you're seeking out to mentor you add value to you? Do they truly possess the skill set you're seeking, or do you just like talking to them? Don't get too hung up on titles. Look for actual, proven skills, experience, and success in the thing you want to learn or know more about.

For instance, a lot of people can mentor you in time management, but if you're fortunate enough to get the CEO's personal administrative assistant to give you tips on scheduling, time management, and getting things done, consider yourself lucky. They're the person managing the calendar of the busiest man/woman in the company. Chances are very good they know what they're talking about.

Likewise, if you're interested in getting and completing a successful project overseas, you might want to seek out someone who has successfully navigated the country that you're going to multiple times. Think outside the box. Do you know anyone in the tourist industry? Who books and manages the flights and takes care of your company's booking and travel issues? If your company doesn't have a dedicated travel department, find a company that does.

Consider what you want to know. Make a list of questions: What happens if you lose your passport? What should I do if the airline loses my luggage? What should I know about officials who insist that I pay bribes or "fines" to travel in their country? There are hundreds of books on how to be a successful global traveler, but actually meeting and being mentored by someone in the travel industry can be very helpful since they'll know things you won't find in books.

My point is that mentors don't have to be executives, C-suite level executives, or the most well-known person in your industry. Mentors are people with the skills and value you need to succeed and progress. They can be motivational speakers, travel agents, foreign language teachers, administrative personnel with an exclusive skillset, taxi drivers, writers, golfers, psychologists, social workers, and parents. Look for the following attributes in your mentors:

- Proven success and an extensive knowledge about the topic or skillset you seek.
- Integrity in what they do and what they share.
- Added value to you, your brand, and your work.
- Empathy. They know or identify with what you're going through.
- Willingness and even eagerness to share their expertise with you.
- Good boundaries. They set healthy boundaries and respect your boundaries.

- Passion for their work and their skills.
- Values learning and growing in their field–they aren't content to rest on their laurels. They like learning no matter how old they are or how long they've been in the industry.
- Honest and realistic feedback–they don't just teach and preach. They observe how you implement what they've shared and give you honest feedback, even if it hurts or stings you to hear it.
- Committed to your success.
- Realistic and well-grounded expectations. They won't tell you that you're CEO material if they don't think you are, yet they will support your dream every way they can.
- A positive and upbeat attitude. Mentors who complain or are negative, critical, and abrasive, are only going to help derail your career, not enhance it.
- A good role model–sets a good example.
- Has the instinct to know when to kick you in the pants and when to extend a helping hand.
- Openness to feedback and challenging questions from you.
- Good communication verbally as well as in written word.
- Good listening skills as well as being a good teacher.
- Respect from their colleagues and co-workers.
- Openness to experimenting with new ideas and

technology.

- Active publications in their industry or field.
- Availability. They are available to you when you need them, either by phone, email or in person. They're not your best friend, on call 24/7, but they do provide a way for you to reach out to them on a reasonable schedule.
- Patience when you struggle.
- Flexibility. They can bend with demands, time, and challenges.
- Respect for you. They treat you as a colleague and professional.

Becoming a mentor

You'll find yourself becoming a mentor to others even when you still feel like you're beginning to learn things yourself. The thing is, there will always be something we do, something that comes easy to us, or something we've always been successful at, that others want to know how to do.

You may be good at networking. Maybe you've never had a problem meeting and talking to new people. For anyone who gets tongue-tied or fears the thought of a conference and the usual networking scene, you may be a great mentor for them.

Maybe you're a whiz at setting and completing goals, creating Gantt charts, speaking on the telephone, organizing events, dealing with distraught people, or navigating a foreign country. Maybe you come from a foreign culture that your colleagues don't understand. You don't have to be the expert. You just have to know what you're doing and be willing to share that with someone who wants to learn. Maybe you once worked on the floor or in manufacturing, and you have a knack with machines or computers. You may be the go-to person people call when something goes wrong. It never hurts to share your knowledge with others. Not only do you expand your network, but you learn how to be a teacher and a mentor. You also improve your brand.

The qualities you'd seek in a mentor also apply to you. When you agree to mentor someone, you're agreeing to be responsible and committed to helping them succeed. That's the difference between answering someone's questions and agreeing to be a mentor.

Mentors take a personal interest in someone learning, applying, and succeeding in incorporating a skill into their job or life. Whether you mentor someone for a few days, a few weeks or forever, you benefit by expanding your network, your value and your connections. If you've been mentored, eventually you'll mentor someone as well. When you do, pay attention to how it feels to be the mentor. Are you respected? Valued? Does your mentee reciprocate time, attention, and value? Just because someone wants to be mentored doesn't mean you have to mentor them.

> Mentoring and being mentored are the lifeblood of any career.

Learn how to mentor and how to be mentored. Either way, successful or not, follow up with your mentor or mentee regularly. Let them know via an email, handwritten card, or phone call, whatever is most appropriate for the relationship, how their help made a difference to you and your career. The one thing anyone hates most about giving advice or help is not hearing back from the person they helped. Mentors want to know they made a difference, and they like knowing their mentees appreciate the help they gave them.

You might need their help down the road, to make an introduction or to give you a positive reference to someone else who may help you. They're less likely to respond favorably if they felt unappreciated.

I've been so fortunate to have had many mentors and to develop so many of those mentoring opportunities into true friendship and valuable networks. Industries are smaller than they may seem, and your brand is everything. It often starts with how well you are mentored and later when you mentor others. The best advice I can give here is, start today. Don't wait to build your mentor network.

The mentoring experience

Not everyone can be a mentor. No matter how you like each other, or enjoy someone's company, they may not be the best mentor for you. Re-read the qualities of a good mentor. What's important to realize is that mentoring and being mentored isn't all good times, roses, and rainbows. If you're being mentored, you're going to fail. Your mentor is going to fail. A good mentor is going to let you fall. They know that's how you learn best. You're going to stumble, hurt yourself, bleed a little, cry, and, maybe, want to quit. A good mentor is going to let you do all those things. They're not there to bubble-wrap you and protect you from the world. They're there to let you experience failure and success, and learn from it. They know you'll learn more from failing and learning to get back up on your feet than you will by being protected and rescued by them. The difference between being a supportive mentor and a rescuer is a fine line for anyone to recognize. Good mentors see that line better than most.

Good mentoring is being able to distinguish between when to extend a helping hand and when to give someone a kick in the pants (or skirt). Good mentors will do both. We learn, grow, and sharpen our skillsets through hearing, doing, and failing. You'll always learn more through a failure than a success. Success feels better of course but when you fail, you learn what not to do as well as what to do.

Mentoring young people

Despite the technological bells, whistles, and smart watches, I think the rules apply to young people just like they did when I was at that age. People who are more senior *enjoy* the opportunity to provide advice and counsel that would be helpful to a young person. They want the young person to show some focus. The mistake I think a lot of young people make is they don't want to miss anything, so they ask for everything. The picture is way too big. "Wow, you're a senior person. Tell me how I can be you one day!" I don't know what to do with that. I've had a whole lot of experiences--made mistakes and tripped up a few times–I can't share or convey my life's experience, wisdom, or insights in five minutes.

Many of today's young people multitask. They think so big, they want to tackle the world, and they don't want to miss *anything*. So, they ask for feedback in as wide-open a way as possible. It's too big, at least for the person who is 10, 15, or 20 years their senior, to address, particularly at a cocktail party, or even in a half hour. I've always encouraged all people, but particularly young people, to be granular. "I noticed in your background, that in the first five years of your career, you were here to here, or doing this and this. Would you help me think through how you made the decision to change jobs?" Or, "I noticed that you went overseas. Tell me why you did that, and what it was that you got out of that." Or, "My personal ambition is to do this in the next five years. What advice would you give me to think about, relative to this, this, and this?" Make the questions and the feedback you request specific, and then you can always stack on top of it, you can bridge, and you can get bigger. If you start really huge then what you get is a really generic answer, as big as the question you asked, and there isn't as much value in that.

Your personal Board of Directors

In the branding chapter we talked about the aspects of your life, of your personality and skill sets, that comprise your brand. There are two halves to it. There are the skills that you need to have as an individual: How do I become a better accountant, a human resources manager, or a lawyer? Like I said, when you're managing your career, that's first and foremost; this doesn't happen if you're not good at what you do.

Then there's the secondary piece, which is really around your ability to navigate, to "play the game," and to understand how to work with and through others. That's actually a skillset in and of itself, but it's one that you develop very differently. A lot of people who say "I don't play politics in the office or workplace" are only hurting themselves. They fail to understand that "playing politics" isn't some sort of game where people lie, deceive, and hurt each other to succeed.

"Playing the game" is about understanding what motivates people, how to motivate people, how to communicate, interact with, and energize and influence people. We all "play the game" with friends and family when we take who they are, and who we are, into consideration before we act or speak. "Playing the game" is simply honing your people skills and using those skills (listening, speaking, inspiring, influencing, comforting, teaching, mentoring, helping, and promoting) to be a successful team player.

That's why I have this whole concept of a personal Board of Directors: a collection of mentors I can turn to for help. By identifying people who can give you advice, counsel, and feedback in many different areas you ensure you aren't blindsided by things you don't know, or didn't see, or haven't learned yet. When you don't know what you don't know, a mentor can be worth their weight in gold, simply because they do know what you don't.

Ask yourself, who can help you build your personal toolkit, your competence, your technical knowledge and abilities? Who can help you with the emotional side, your ability to feel energized, and confident and excited? Who can help you with the politics and decisions about whom to influence and whom to connect and partner with, whom to fight against–when to lean into those emotions and when not? Who looks at you and builds you up? Who looks at you in order to really challenge you, when you need that? I think you need the whole thing, and it's hard to find all that from one or two mentors. That's why I've always believed in a collection of mentors with very purposeful roles for each of them, in terms of how they guide me. When I have that, then I'm able to tap into them at different times, depending upon what I'm dealing with or managing.

It would be difficult to count the mentors I have now, but I would say easily twelve or fifteen. That doesn't include all the mentors I've had throughout my life. In addition to those golden twelve or fifteen, there are others I might tap into for a specific question or query. Maybe I know someone in an industry, or organization who I don't have a lot of contact with, or who I don't know too much about. Having a mentor, someone who is in that industry, or who knows the ropes, can save me a lot of time and energy. As I always say, mentorship can be as little as thirty minutes and a cup of coffee, depending on what is needed. I could be at a cocktail party and bump into somebody. So, for those thirty minutes, I share two or three things I'd like to know, that they might have insight about, and that will make me smarter about a topic that I don't know much about.

Mentoring the C-suite

For those with aspirations into the C-suite, you do want to get to a point where you start to scrutinize your personal Board of Directors. There should be a subset of that broader board, hopefully, that emerges as your inner circle–I refer to it as my kitchen cabinet–that can help you with the increased level of scrutiny, navigation skills, and insights required to crack the C-suite, to crack into the Board of Directors.

Here, it's not as much about the technical aspects of what you deliver. The assumption is that everybody at those levels is pretty good. It's more about the relationships, the brand that you're positioning. It's about the leverage that you can create or enable, so that a person will want to invest in you and will say, "We want to bring you into the senior team," or "We want to bring you into the C-suite," or "We want to put you on the executive committee," and eventually, "We want to put you on our Board."

Not everyone can advise you there. A lot of people want to give you advice or think they can give you advice. I'll give you an example. I was giving a career talk, and there was a person making kind of a snippy statement. He said, "Oh, Orlando, he's got that big job, but you know he had to kiss a lot of ass to get that job. I'm not an ass-kisser, so that's why I'm not going to be there."

I'll be honest: There are things you need to manage and navigate, but there are a lot of myths about what it takes.

Make your impact on the company and make your brand part of your messaging. It's not just about who's boss right now. Because if you do kiss a lot of a particular individual's butt as the way to navigate to the top, well, that person could quit or leave or do something different, and now you're hung out there to dry. I wouldn't see that as a strategy for migration into the C-suite at all. That's my opinion. But, a lot of people, because there's this mystery about what it takes to get into the C-suite, or this mystery about the executive floor, take their own misperceptions, insecurities, fears, and then try to apply those to other people. So, you have to be careful who you take advice from when you think about those big jobs. Take it all with a grain of salt–meaning consider the source and their possible agenda, experience, or point of view and how close, or not, it is to yours.

You have to ask for it

I started being aware of when I needed support from others in high school. I would see things and make observations, and I would ask questions–whether as a student in school or in my internships. I always found adults were very helpful and would respond well to a young person. You could ask almost anything, and they would not only give you an answer, but would even discuss the answer with you if you wanted.

I think I turned this awareness into conscious competence when I was in graduate school, and I was trying to figure out where I wanted to work. I would talk to people and call people. There are some people who are friends and mentors today who I met way back then. For instance, while I was in college a lot of alumni would come back and speak to the classes. I found it powerful for a person five or ten years older than I was, who had been out in the work world and was back, to talk about their work experiences

More than just sitting there awestruck though, I would always follow up. I would meet the person after the presentation. I would ask if they would mind if I called them and asked them some questions, and I would do that. I would set up a call and then talk on the phone with them for half an hour.

Some of those phone calls have blossomed into relationships that still exist today. There's a guy by the name of Shawn Taylor who went to Purdue. I met Shawn when I was in college. He was coming back to speak, and I was still a graduate student trying to figure out what I wanted to do next. He worked for Arthur Andersen. (I ended up working for Andersen Consulting.) Then he went off and became an entrepreneur and wildly successful, while I did the corporate thing. He was, and is, a very successful businessperson and entrepreneur. He retired at the age of 46.

Throughout the years we stayed friends. He's been a close friend and mentor for more than twenty years now and we belong to the same golf clubs, we travel together, and our families spend time together. When I have issues around finance or jobs or things of that nature, I call him. He's expanded his network to be helpful to me, he's taken me to his summer home. and invited some other pretty affluent people to give me coaching and guidance on corporate careers. He's been wonderful, and when I went to visit him in Houston, he hosted a dinner and invited his network–a kind of "Who's Who in Houston"–who he thought would be good resources for me, and me for them. Not all mentors become close friends like Shawn and I have become, but some do.

Turning the tables

I'd say that I started giving back well before I was established in any kind of career. When I was in college, Purdue would send me off to other schools to help recruit students for the graduate program. Companies that were interested in me also had me serve as a recruiter, even while I was still in school. I've always had that spirit of advice, counsel, sales, and storytelling, and I started giving back pretty early. It's just a skill set and character trait that has expanded over the years.

As I've had more to share, I've been able to offer more. In college, I went back and talked to my high school's students. When I graduated from college, I went back and talked to college students. As I grew in my career, I'd talk to high schoolers, then college kids, and now corporate people. I'd look back at where I was and see if I had anything to offer those whose place I'd just occupied not so long ago.

As a mentor, I think you're a better receiver, and you receive more, if you're a better giver. When you go to a networking situation, those who go there to give actually end up getting more than those that go to get. It's just a rule of life. Whether it's serendipity or the ethos, people are more apt to give to a person who's giving as well. It's just how it works. Shawn and I are a great example of that. He's so helpful to me, so I make it a point to try to be helpful to him. It's almost like we have a competition to see who can give more to the other person.

It's simple things. He was at Purdue recently, and he called me. "Hey, Orlando, do you want a hat, a shirt?" I was like, "Sure!" So, he grabbed a hat and a shirt and put it in the mail to me. He didn't just send it to me, he overnighted it. He didn't need to do that, I wasn't in a rush for it. But it was a nice touch.

When he's in Chicago, he wants to go play golf. I belong to a golf club in Chicago so I'm likely to say, "Hey, why don't you play at my club?" I set it up and then I tell them, "Look–make sure you don't charge him. Put it on my account." Because, I want to reciprocate his kindness with my kindness. That's just our relationship. He gives, I give. I believe whether it's mentoring or anything else, that's just a good approach.

Another important point, whether you are the mentor or the mentee, but particularly if you have a mentee. Have a point of view. Have some clarity around what that point of view is and be willing to articulate it. It doesn't mean that it's right, it doesn't mean that everything you say as a mentor is the gospel truth and that that person should execute it, the value comes from having a clear and concise point of view. Even as a mentee, you should have a point of view. What is it that you're trying to get from the conversation? What do you want to be when you grow up?

The most painful mentor-mentee discussions are when the mentee just sort of shows up and says, "So... tell me. What should I do? Give me guidance." That's not how it works. How would I even respond to that? "Well, here's ten years of my experience, see what you can do with that." No, that's just not helpful.

If I have something to work with then I can help. The more granular your needs are, the more granular my advice can be. That's where the value comes. If you say, "I want to be vice president of my area of expertise in the next ten years, and here's where I am today; what do you think I need to do in order to achieve that?" Then I can say, "Well, here's what I know. Boom, boom, boom. But here's what I don't know, and here's somebody who can give you that information and help you with the parts that you don't know."

That's how I've ended up with additional mentors as well. I've always tried to be really specific. "Here's what I'm looking for: X, Y, and Z." And, my mentor would always say, "Okay, well, I know this and this and this–but man, I don't know those other three parts. Here's the person who does." Then you talk to that other person, and they say, "Here's the person who knows the next piece." The next thing you know, you've got four, five, six people out there looking at your challenge, as opposed to just the one.

Diversity of insight

What I'm trying to help you build is a diversity of advice that helps you have a richer set of insights. I *don't* think there's any magic in getting started in building a personal Board of Directors or finding a mentor. I think you just have to live and be curious, and as you do that, you'll find opportunities. Keep asking yourself, what don't I know? When you ask yourself that question, I think you're going to find the questions you will ask others. If you know what you don't know, and know what you want or need to know, then you can turn to people. Then you can build out your set of granular questions. Make a list of the things you don't know, that you want to know more about, and then get more and more specific around the questions. Then of course there are the concrete things to ask about. What to read, where to go for the trade shows or industry events, or do I go back to school?

For example, this is how I met Don Thompson, the former CEO of McDonald's. Don was named Purdue Black Alum one year, and then the following year, I was named Purdue Black Alum. He heard about my award through Purdue's marketing of the event, so, he came to see my speech out of support and curiosity. He said, "Hey, I'd heard a lot about you, and I'd heard good things, and I decided I wanted to come so I could meet you." I was touched by that comment, because I knew who he was. We began a friendship at that event that continues to this day, and he is an important person on my personal Board of Directors. Always do your best, and others will notice and will be willing to give out and give back to you.

As a minority, finding the right mentors can be a matter of belonging to organizations that promote those kinds of connections. For example, there are lots African American professional groups inside organizations and outside organizations, which are meant to do just that. I belong to The Executive Leadership Council (The ELC), which has provided me with people who looked like me, and who understood the nuances, the challenges, and extraordinary things about corporate America. They serve as a collection of mentors, mentees, and people who I can mentor as well around lots of different topics and subjects in the executive suite. By getting involved in those organizations–being a giver–there is a bunch that you will get back.

Every time I have a speaking engagement, every time I give a presentation, or every time I go and meet with some young people, my intentions are to go there to be helpful. Very often I'll meet someone who will end up being helpful to me as well. It's happened to me consistently throughout my career. Give and you will receive.

Sponsorship

This is the ultimate business relationship where a person stakes their personal reputation, vote of confidence, and belief in you, and will advocate on your behalf for a role or position or opportunity. Sponsors are relationships that evolve where a person decides upon seeing you perform and then develops a personal connection before they decide to act as a sponsor.

Throughout my career I have had numerous people ask me to sponsor them. However, if you ask me to be a sponsor for you and I don't have any idea as to how you work, how can I do that? I can give you advice and perhaps mentor you, but I can't advocate for you without time and the development of first a networking and then a mentoring relationship.

I've had several sponsors over my career. All of them evolved. I didn't ask. I didn't even know they were my sponsor until they put their influence behind me in support of a major development or job opportunity. I like to think I have developed a strong professional reputation and in several different scenarios these individual sponsors have given me stretch opportunities and sponsored me. These sponsorship opportunities have helped my career tremendously.

The million-dollar question for you would be, *how* do you get a sponsor. Whereas the sponsor relationship is cultivated over time with perceived successful performance on your part, it is best for you to look to your current mentor to nurture this important relationship. Of course, if you don't have a mentor at this time, start seeking one out.

Building your network

Long before they knew what the words "network" or "networking" means, most people were already doing it. I was no different.

As I mentioned earlier, I was born in Maine, lived in Pennsylvania, New Jersey, and Georgia, and attended school in Indiana. I moved around a lot as a kid, so I learned at an early age about the power of integrating by creating relationships and making connections through social skills. I didn't call it the power of networking. Odds are I didn't even know what '"networking" was–but I learned how to make friends, fit in, and figure out how to culturally swing fast because I was the new kid. I had to figure it out if I wanted to survive.

I am black, born in an all-white environment, and have lived in all-black environments too. I have also lived in racially integrated situations. I've lived in the North, the South, the Midwest, and overseas. These were all very different cultures. Eventually, I developed an ability to connect with people. I think it was something that I did as a self-preservation skill, in order to belong. That skill naturally translated into networking–where the ability to create connections and blend in translated into the relationships that had mutual benefits and value.

I spent three years of my youth in Georgia where I experienced all-white spaces, all-black spaces, and spaces that were being integrated for the first time. The transformational moment for me in learning to navigate all of those spaces was when the two schools were integrated, and I became class president of the mixed school in the seventh grade.

At the time, I lived with my northern family in an all-white neighborhood in the Deep South. Then, at the beginning of the seventh grade, they implemented busing, and I got bused to the all-black school on the other side of town.

I think what I was able to do there was develop comfort playing in multiple cultural settings. At the end of the day, while there were lots of differences between these two groups at the integrated school (and most of the kids were focusing on the differences), there were clearly lots of things we had in common. We were all in seventh grade. We were all young people, and we all liked recess and chocolate milk at lunch. It helped that we probably weren't so fond of the boring biology teacher. Rather than try to fix the points where we differed, I tried to focus on the points of commonality when I ran for president. I guess that made a difference.

One of the key skills to career success is emotional intelligence or people skills, and it's more than just being friendly and smiling. That's part of it, but it's really about knowing how to find common ground with individuals. It's a game I like to play, actually. And, because I've lived around the world and traveled extensively, I have more tools to be able to do that. When I meet a new group of people and we go around, I can usually connect with a person on something within three questions. "Tell me about yourself, where are you from, and where were you born." It's not uncommon that I've either worked in or visited their home town.

Owning it

The other thing that made a difference came from a choice I made about something totally beyond my control. Not only am I an African American male but usually the only tall, African American male in the room. There are two ways I could respond to those situations. I could shy away from them by toning myself down in an effort to blend into the room, or I can *lean into* these circumstances. I usually choose to lean into them. I have a big voice and a big laugh as well. People notice me. My demeanor gives me a window to introduce myself, and take others away from wondering, "Who is that guy," or making assumptions about me.

Hopefully, I can quickly move them to where I want them to be, which is, "Wow, that's an insightful senior executive." Most of the initial assumptions people sometimes have about me are that I'm a professional athlete, limo driver, or bodyguard. I want to take them from "Who's that guy? He must be a bodyguard," to "Wow, *this* is who he is," and being intrigued and interested in who I really am. By doing that, I can create the connection I want. It's through that movement from "Who" and "What" to "Oh, wow," that the magic begins.

Creating that connection, no matter how you do it, is where you have the opportunity to build your network. If you spend all your effort trying to tone and pat down your differences, well, then people aren't going to pay attention to who you really are. I think you miss out on opportunities to connect when you're trying to please and soothe others. Connecting over what makes you and the other person unique is what creates the network.

Even my name is something that's helped me. There aren't a lot of Orlandos in the world. The most famous ones are in Shakespeare, Woolf, and Florida. So, people remember my name, and partly because of it, people remember what I say. They remember seeing me. I was in the airport lounge recently waiting for a flight and a young woman approached me. She asked, "Is your name Orlando Ashford?" I said yes and she said, "I remember you. You spoke at the National Black MBA conference in Houston two years ago." And she proceeded to recall in detail what I'd spoken about. She brought out her phone and brought up the notes she had taken from the presentation I had made that day, and she began reiterating the points.

We were able to sit and talk, and make a new connection, and I was able to add her more formally to my network. I made the initial investment in that connection–without even knowing it would result in a connection–simply by being different and compelling. She obviously remembered me well enough to want to interact with me and connect. That happens to me quite a bit.

It just takes one to make a difference

I know it was grade school, but let's go back to Georgia when I was class president. I think I got there not because of any one particular connection, but because I was open to connecting with *everyone*, black or white. I actually ended up being a bit of a bridge between the two different "cultures," if you will, being African American but bused from a white neighborhood. I was also from the Northeast, which made me different in a way that was unique to everybody. Yet, I could find ways to connect to everybody while also being different from everybody, which actually helped me find common ground.

One incident during my time at the all-white school really stands out for me. I used to get into a lot of fights with a particular, small group of kids. Every week or so, five or six of them would jump me, to the point that I got pretty good at fighting groups of kids. It's not a skillset that I recommend, but I learned how to be pretty good at it. After these fights, no matter what–win, lose, or draw–I always showed back up.

Whatever happened–good, bad, or indifferent–I showed back up at school. I was a good student. I was very smart. I got good grades, and even though I had these incidents, I would always show back up.

There was one kid who was always there named Ross. He was kind of a bigger, redheaded kid. This one particular day, the kids were assembling to mess with me, and Ross was in the group. But this time, he stepped out of the group, stood next to me and said, "If you're going to fight him, you're going to fight me, too." That was the last day I got jumped. It just took one person standing by my side to change things.

We're in the era of having hundreds of friends on sites like Facebook. Many of us seek out as many people as we can when all it really takes is just one person willing to stand by us to make our network real. It just takes one person to make a difference in a young person's career. It just takes one to stop a kid from getting jumped every week. You can find that one, or you can be that one. And, you can do both.

Making the connection

When people describe me, they use words such as energetic, charismatic, and fun. I had a boss who also described me as having a natural, inherent ability to connect with people. He said I was the kind of person for whom people would quickly develop an affinity or connection. That trait has been helpful in creating relationships with a variety of people, including those who would go on to become my mentors, people willing to invest in me, and people who would give me advice and counsel. As I've gotten older, and more senior, that ability to connect has translated into having sponsors who are willing to go on the line for me and say, "You know, I think this person, this young kid, this gentleman, has what it takes to go to the next step, or further." They had trust in me, so they've been public with that and created opportunities for me that accelerated my career.

I have a lot of valuable skill sets, experience, and knowledge, but it all started with the ability to create *genuine* connections with people. A key word here is genuine. I honestly like people. I don't fake it. I think I'm naturally a giving person and a social person. For those reasons, I've been able to create natural connections pretty easily. People can sense the real deal, the genuine article. You can't fake that kind of energy.

I'd also say it's created some negative relationships. One of the things I had to get used to, as I got more senior and successful, is that there are people out there who will not like you. Either they're jealous of, intimidated, or upset by you in some way. They may see you as a threat. Perhaps they sense some competition, or they differ from you philosophically, and would take the opposite approach. Even though I'd like to think I've always been nice to everyone, it doesn't always play out positively. Someone once said, "If you're waiting for everybody to like you, you're going to be waiting a hell of a long time." It's the unfortunate truth that as you ascend up the corporate ladder, you will create enemies, even if that isn't your intention.

It happens because people have other ambitions, and they see your success as a threat to them, so they may take a negative posture toward you. I've come to realize that it's just part of the deal. At every company I've worked, I've had an "arch-enemy" (in big scary quotes), a peer who saw me as competition, or as a threat rather than a friend or asset, and who took a negative posture toward me. I used to think it was me, and maybe I wasn't doing something right, I wasn't nice enough, or I had done something to the person or offended them somehow. Eventually, I realized I hadn't done anything to the person. I was just being successful.

Build a network that's right for you

All networks are not the same, and that's a good thing. In fact, the more networks you have, the better. For instance, I used to play basketball in high school and college, and I still play a decent game of pick-up. Earlier in my career, when I would travel internationally, I would try to find where the local gym was–where the best players were in that particular country–and I would show up as an American. Despite not necessarily knowing the language, let alone these guys' names, I would have a great time. It was unusual, because there would be some local gym, and some guy (me) would just pop in, and they would welcome me into the game. I was pretty good, so I could hold my own, and in the process, I ended up creating relationships and networks that gave me access in the country in a much more local, personal way, than if I'd gone to my hotel gym. It's an example of a way to gain different perspectives from the local community wherever you are.

Vacations are great, and you should absolutely see the usual tourist sites. See the Eiffel Tower, the Great Pyramid, and Angkor Wat. But as you try to globalize, try to find a way to get a more local experience in a way that's genuine and personal to you. For me, that connection was basketball. For somebody else, it could be art or music, golf or scuba diving, bird watching or museums. When I was an ex-patriot and lived in Turkey, my family and I made a conscious decision to live in a much more local neighborhood. There were ex-patriot compounds, where people from Western Europe and the U.S. would congregate in an attempt to recreate a more Western lifestyle, and there's nothing wrong with that. It certainly helps to acclimate while you're learning to navigate the country, speak the language, and keep from feeling so homesick.

However, we were trying to get a real dose of the local experience. So, we were in a much smaller compound. When we went to the local butcher, the local baker, the local grocery store, we had a much more local experience. Certainly, it created some challenges because we didn't know the language or the culture, but it also created some wonderful learning experiences. I know one of the reasons my children are as global as they are today is because of that experience. They were two and seven when we were there, so they're both very comfortable traveling on a plane. They are now 15 and 20, both know multiple languages, and they're comfortable with people who look, act, dress, and speak differently than they do. As the world becomes more interconnected, I think it'll be important for people to challenge themselves and embrace differences.

Today, the media often does the world a complete disservice in how they paint the picture of what's going on in the world. When I traveled from Turkey back to the U.S., my friends in the U.S. would say, "I bet you're glad to be back in the U.S.–where it's safe." Then, when I traveled back to Turkey, my Turkish friends would say, "I bet you're glad to be back here in Turkey–where it's safe." The only news that you would see about either country is the bad news! The U.S. media depicted bombings and soldiers up in the mountains, looking for people, and the Turkish media showed shootings in American cities or at schools. Both sides would see the most extreme violence of the other side, shaping their perception of the other country and its people. As a result, there were people on both sides who wanted nothing to do with the other side, and they were both missing out on what I saw and experienced as the real Turkey and the real America.

Compound that effect. When violence, strife, and difference are all you see on the news around the world, you don't get any other perspective on what's really happening. You only see the bad news. Every country has problems, but every country also has its brilliance, beauty, people, food, music, and life. Most of us are scared to go find and experience it.

Not everyone can live abroad, but if you can, you really should. If you can't move, then travel (when we are safe from a pandemic and borders are open), but then, when you travel, remember there are different ways to travel. You could treat your ex-patriot or international travel experience like the zoo, where you experience another culture from the other side of a protective barrier. Or, another way is to actually get *in* it, and say, "Wow, that looks like fun." Hang out, and meet and get to know some people, which is what I've always tried to do in some way.

If I have time, that's how I always prefer to travel. It doesn't have to be anything elaborate. I have a buddy from Dubai who I met while I was there. We went to a Lebanese restaurant for dinner. He knew the owner, and some of the local guys. The whole dinner was done in Arabic, and my buddy interpreted the dinner and evening conversation for me. I had such a great time that I went back the next night and just hung out with the owner and the same group of guys by myself, without my buddy to interpret. I got so comfortable reading body language and doing pantomime, that spoken language wasn't even necessary for enjoyment.

One thing to consider, too, is that different cultures embrace other races and cultures differently. As an African American, I'm actually embraced differently in, say, the Middle East than other Americans. In some of these places–they know American history, but they also sometimes know *black* American history. Sometimes you get credit for that. They don't really like Americans, but sometimes they'll appreciate Black Americans because they see us as having been oppressed.

The first time I went to the Middle East, I was nervous. I had an American passport, and I didn't know how I was going to be treated. I got up to the front of the line at Bahrain immigration and the passport control employee said, "Ah, brother, welcome home." He let me through and brought my entire family water. Again, with hundreds of people in line, he brought nothing to anyone else. I was the only black person in line, and it was an open door. He smiled, asked us questions, and invited us into many aspects of his community. He was totally different than when he stamped our passports and went to the next person—*wsssh*. He went right back to the stoic face. "Next." I was there as an American, but they were seeing me as a Black American. Because they understood the history of slavery in the U.S., they gave me credit for it.

Leveraging recruiters

One member of your career community that you might not think of is the recruiter or headhunter. These people and organizations are valuable resources that literally track and follow your progress throughout your entire career. They know what's happening in the job market and they have a great handle on the value of your skills and experiences in that market. Knowing your worth is extremely powerful. It helps you understand if you're being treated fairly in your current role and also in making smart decisions about any desired career moves. I have relationships with recruiters going back more than 20 years. They have helped me find new opportunities, they've provided advice as I've considered career opportunities, and they've helped me understand my fair compensation value when considering a new job or promotion. In order to receive this value, I invested in these relationships. I've been a resource for them with references and potential candidates for jobs they were trying to fill. One recruiter friend was going out on his own and I helped him think through his business strategy and even the name of his firm. Are you catching my point? The executive search firm and recruiter is a powerful resource that can be extremely helpful as you navigate your career journey.

Many people make the mistake of not paying attention to recruiters until they need them, but at that point you are at a disadvantage. They don't know you and that lack of history puts you lower on the consideration list. I've asked my former colleague and friend Michelle Sutter, who has a background in executive search to share a few perspectives on how to leverage recruiters in your career journey.

Opening the door to your professional future–Your quick guide to leveraging recruiters and creating opportunity in a competitive market.

It's a highly competitive job market out there, and candidates today are more educated than ever before. Globalization has made it possible to get a job anywhere across the world. And while the current workforce of highly skilled candidates is incredibly competitive, the number of new jobs remains stagnant.

For many employers, the outlandish cost of turnover has forced a new heightened focus on employee retention–starting with the hiring process. As such, many employers today work with recruiters to seek out, vet, and hire high-quality candidates in an attempt to make the perfect hire while minimizing the potential profit-pitfalls of organizational turnover.

As a jobseeker, it is critical to follow these basic steps in order to effectively work with a recruiter and maximize your opportunity to open the door to a career that you find fulfilling and financially rewarding.

1. Understand your value: Take the time to understand your value proposition and how it can directly pertain to the needs of the organization the recruiter has been hired by. A relationship with a recruiter can help you assess your market value as they see hundreds of people and backgrounds

2. Mind your social media: Many recruiters will take the time to do a deep dive on your social media presence and any other online information. It is critical to be mindful of what you post and ensure that your information is as locked up as possible. For content that is not locked up, maintain a professional demeanor that is free of any potential red flags.

3. Invest in building your LinkedIn: More than 90 percent of recruiters use LinkedIn when exploring a potential candidate, and a stunning 20 million employers present on the platform. So, keeping your LinkedIn up-to-date, fresh, and eye-catching is critical.

4. Don't snub recruiters: It's the nature of the game: Sometimes recruiters will invite you to explore an opportunity that is not a good fit for you. It is important to not dismiss the recruiter, but instead, use it as an opportunity to network with them and encourage them to keep you in mind for future roles. You never know what great job opportunity could present itself in the future if you take the time to engage in a meaningful interaction with the recruiter.

5. Be ready to refer: If you discover the job is not a good fit for you, create new networking opportunities and build rapport with the recruiter. Be ready to refer a colleague or other candidate who you feel would be a better fit. This helps build a relationship of trust and reliability with the recruiter.

6. Respond quickly and be available: Recruiters are juggling a lot–and they don't have time for follow-up. Respond to messages quickly and make yourself available for interviews whenever they offer.

7. Ask for feedback: If you don't secure the position, be humble, gracious, and ask for constructive feedback on how to improve. This will help you for the next opportunity.

8. Be direct: Ask the recruiter bluntly if there are any potential concerns they have regarding your candidacy that you can address. Also inquire about your market value and competitiveness as a candidate. This will allow you to offset any concerns while building rapport with the recruiter.

9. Ask for the job: Simply interviewing for a job doesn't imply that you want it. If you truly want the position, ask for it directly.

10. Be passionate: Often, the most experienced or qualified candidate doesn't get the job; the most passionate, hungrier, and committed candidate does. Be vocal about your value set and then put it all out on the line.

The employment market is tough, but by working well with recruiters, you can truly open the door on endless opportunities for the future.

Mentors, sponsors, and apprentices

I've been really lucky with having great mentors and sponsors. Now that I'm more advanced in my career, I see it as my responsibility to turn around and be a mentor and a sponsor for others. When it comes to what I do for others, there are three levels of assistance, because I couldn't possibly mentor every young person who asks.

The first level is what I'll call general advice and counsel. I do a lot of public speaking on the topic of careers, my specific career path, and certain areas of expertise that people like to hear about. For instance, I'm on a publicly traded Board, and people often will ask me to come and talk about what it's like to sit on a Board, or how they themselves can get on a Board. So, I'll speak about that or careers more generally. I give at least twenty presentations a year, maybe more, on various topics, and that's not including the work I have done inside my own company. I do a decent amount of speaking. Hopefully, people will learn and gain value from the advice that I give when I speak.

The next level has more to do with actually being a one-time mentor. Oftentimes, either coming from those presentations or elsewhere, people will ask for a specific time to focus on their specific career and their issues. I will have a 30-minute cup of coffee with 20-25 people over the course of a year for a more formal session.

The third level is a subset of people that I will "shepherd," directly mentor, or sponsor on an ongoing basis. This is clearly a smaller group, but these are the people that I will either have hired myself or that I help position into jobs with other people.

When I get calls about job opportunities, there's a small subset of people that I will refer for them if they're opportunities for which I feel they'd make a really good fit and I can personally attest to their capability related to that job. In that case, I will try to position those people in those opportunities. If I change jobs, and there are people who I've hired, I'll try to make sure that they're okay and doing well at the company where I'm leaving them, or I'll try to take them with me to the new company. In some cases, I'll try to reposition them at another company. That's part of the sponsorship relationship.

It's unfortunate that few people are equally generous with their relationships and with their positioning and helping of others. Most people that I see sponsor a person or two, and only in their own area of expertise. I don't think a lot of people sponsor the way I do, which does take quite a bit of time. But I want to encourage more people to do what I'm doing, because I think it's critical.

In Europe, these kinds of sponsorship relationships are much more developed, usually in the form of apprenticeships. You see them in professional kitchens, in companies, in the military–everywhere. In many armies abroad, for instance, people who are looking to get into leadership positions actually apprentice to get those positions. Apprenticeships are different from internships in that you're basically teaching an individual *everything* they could, or really should know about a position. So, it's not just a particular project that they're working on. They're actually creating their career from the ground up through learning on the job, about the job, from a master or expert.

If you were my apprentice and I taught you everything that you know about a topic, then I might flip to being your sponsor, thinking, "Well, they're as good at their job as I am. I taught them everything they know." However, because we don't have those relationships anymore–not formally–it rarely happens. I can think of several people for whom this kind of relationship is true.

When I was at Motorola, I was the head of organizational development, and my right-hand person, Jenn, worked with me for several years. When I left Motorola to work at Coca-Cola, I then hired her at Coca-Cola. So, she followed me to Coca-Cola.

And she's a brilliant organizational development consultant–one of the best. I can't take credit for her success because she is responsible for that herself–she's wonderfully talented–but I've definitely influenced her development, her career, and her ambitions. She's has since left Coca-Cola and has gone on to become CHRO and then COO of Dollar Shave Club.

We've also talked about working together again at some point. She's somebody that I continue to sponsor, even though she's doing well where she is. And when people call me and ask, "Who's the best in this field?" she's one of the names that I give. If I were to start a company from scratch, she's one of the people I would hire. That apprenticeship-type relationship definitely exists, because I had and still have a pulse on her, in terms of her professional development and also personally, because we're friends.

Get in the game

Another friend whom I sponsor is very talented and works really hard, but in my opinion, he works too hard. What I mean by that is, he puts all of his energy and effort into delivering and executing the work. You have to be talented, and you have to deliver the goods, but you also have to invest in relationships. People need to know you and like you, particularly as you aspire to those more senior roles. So, you can be as talented as you want to be, but--if you don't show up at the events, if you don't have a network so that when people say, "Hey, this opportunity came up," and your name comes to mind–it doesn't make a difference how good you are. If you want to be a player in the game, you have to be *in* the game. This is what I call *table* stakes.

When I invite him to events, his usual response is, "Man, I would love to come, but I'm too busy." I get really upset with him, because then, two weeks later he'll complain, "Man, I'm missing out on opportunities. My career's not progressing the way I want." And, I say, "That's because you don't invest in your network! You don't invest in relationships! People don't know you! You're at work, so the only people who are happy are your direct boss and those people who work around you. Which is a good thing, and will allow you to keep a job, but that doesn't allow your career to flourish. Those are two different things."

A lot of times people will do the things that allow them to keep a job. There's nothing wrong with that. Keeping a job is important; it enables you to have an income, pay the rent, and eat. But, if you're trying to foster a career, you have to have relationships beyond just your one job. Particularly in today's business environment where things change so quickly.

I had a boss once tell me, "In order to be successful, Orlando, you've got to really go all-in in the job that you have. You've got to forego other relationships, other areas of interest, and go 110 percent on the one job that you have." I think that is the absolute worst idea and advice possible, particularly in today's business environment, because things change so quickly. If I go in 110 percent at my one job, with my one boss, but there's a change in the strategy and my boss is gone, then what do I have to stand on? I'm not saying you shouldn't work hard or that you shouldn't get stuff done. Absolutely, you have to do that, but you also have to take some time to invest in broader relationships outside of just the one that you have.

The image I like to use is that you should be playing on three chess boards at the same time. The one chess board is the job that you have today. You want to be smart, put in time and effort–in fact, that's your priority. That's the chess game that you're in right now, but you should have some pieces on two other chess boards. Periodically, you need to look up, slide your chair over to the left, and make a move on your other chess board. And, again periodically, you need to look up, slide to the right, and make a move on your third chess board. If something happens in the game that you're playing, you're not stuck. That's something that I've made a point of always doing.

Some would say that it has limited me. I say, wherever I was, I've never felt limited. If you looked at the structure of my career, I'd argue just the opposite I think playing three boards has made me a better executive. I've been able to be bolder in my current chess game–because I knew if this blew up I had opportunities on chess boards two and three. People, who only play one chess board, are often scared and they don't make strong moves. These people can actually become vindictive and competitive, and I think those are the people who ended up being my arch enemies whenever I would show up.

Because, remember, I would move from company to company. I would parachute into a new organization, and there would be a person sitting there who had been there for 10, 15, even 20 years. They may think: "Who's this guy, parachuting into this big role? Why does everyone like and connect with him, and why are they promoting him and moving him into these bigger roles? I've got to get him, because he's getting the work or promotion I've been waiting for the last 20 years."

This is why I tell people, "Don't' play defensively in your careers. Engage in the building of your network muscle." Those arch enemies weren't building anything. They were just defending what they had, and as a result, they never gained any new territory.

If you ask people who work for me what they enjoy about it, they may explain that I can be serious and funny at the same time. I get things done, but I don't take myself too seriously, so I can laugh at myself and others. You don't want to take yourself too seriously, and you should try to create environments where there's enjoyment along the way. I can be in some of the most intense situations and still find a moment to laugh. The ability to share a laugh and a connection, no matter who you are in the room with, is a critical skill–for success in your *career*, and also for success in life.

Quality, not quantity

When I was in high school, I was kind of a nerd. I had friends, but I didn't have lots of friends. I wasn't necessarily the coolest kid. Remember, I was the one interning at AT&T over the summer, not scoring touchdowns. So, when I went to college, I was on a mission to become a Cool Kid with a capital C, and I was very purposeful about changing my presence and image.

And, I was successful. I became very popular. I knew everyone on campus and had a huge contact list. I went to a lot of the parties, and I was very social. Soon I realized, though, that the volume of people did not replace the quality of the connections. As a result, as I've progressed through my career, I've always focused more on quality than quantity. I have lots of acquaintances; I know lots of people, clearly. That comes with my work. Those who I would call friend, trusted adviser, or on my Board of Directors… I reserve that for a select few.

Don't burn your bridges

If I think back, there are probably four or five people who played critical roles in making my career, including someone I worked with at Motorola. I was the head of organizational development, and he ran HR. When I started to work for him–I'll never forget this–he told me, "We'll know within six months whether you're going to work out or not." Basically, I was on probation with him for my first six months. And, literally to the *day*, six months later, he said, "You're pretty good. You can stay."

And, slowly, the relationship began to change. I read an old Harvard Business Review article called, "A Letter to My White Boss." I thought, "I'll give it to my boss. He's white; I'm black." It discussed how to manage a person of color, including some ideas or tips and distinctions, some things that your white boss might not think about. I put the article in his inbox and never heard back from him.

Perhaps two months later, he came to my office and he said, "You know, there's an African American on the board. I've talked to him about maybe being a mentor to you. Would you find that valuable?" To which I said, "Absolutely. I'd appreciate that." And, he said, "Great. Well, I'll make that happen." Then he said, "I got that idea from that article you gave me two months ago." It created a kind of bond between us, a relationship. He stayed a friend and a mentor well after I left Motorola, and he has served on my personal Board of Directors ever since.

I had a similar situation with a guy named David Nadler. He hired me at Delta Consulting, back in 1999 when it was his firm. I worked with him for about four years. Then, we were acquired, became Mercer Delta, and I became a partner. I was the youngest partner, the only African American at the time, and I was on a great trajectory. David put a lot of pressure on me, saying things like, "Why are you doing this? I don't know if this is the best move," and so on.

When I gave notice to work for Mercer Consulting, I told him, "I want to make sure I leave you in a good way. Whatever I was working on, whatever you need me to do, I'll take care of it, so this goes smoothly." So, I did double duty for a little while to try to make sure I left in a good way, because I said, "Life and careers are long, and I think we'll have the opportunity to work together again." Fast forward seven years, when I was recruited back to Marsh & McLennan's company to be the head of HR.

The person who put my name on the radar for that opportunity was David Nadler.

He was vice chairman and the company wanted somebody who was different and would bring some new energy to the job. David said, "You know, this guy who used to work for me–I'm not sure where he is now..." The search firm found me. I was in Turkey, and I got recruited from Turkey back for this opportunity. The point being, having a couple of people willing to sponsor you and put energy behind you is something that we're all going to need. This is particularly so as you aspire to some of those senior-level roles in the C-suite.

All of those tips are important–building a good brand, being reputable, and delivering, but so is having people like you, being conscious of how you show up, and how you leave.

> Leave with the door open behind you. You don't want to burn bridges. You want to be conscious and put as much effort around how you leave as there is around how you enter.

When you leave, you've got a new opportunity, and you're excited about it. You might be frustrated with the old place, or somebody pissed you off. Even so, you want to be conscious of leaving in the best way you can. When you're leaving in a negative situation, whatever the reason, make it as great and gracious of an exit as you made an entrance.

The big lesson

Don't go around wearing a chip on your shoulder. Connection, if created well, creates benefits for both parties. It's one thing to connect and get a short, quick win with somebody, like when they help you get a good table at a restaurant. It's another thing to have a network who can help you in more substantial ways, such as an interview with the best company in the field right now. The idea is to create a sustainable network that continuously pays you back. You contribute to them, and they contribute back to you. It may be a cliché, but "Win-Win" is a fact of making a good personal or work life.

Everything plays in your brand. Everything plays in the story that you're trying to create and trying to tell. Depending on your aspirations, and how bad you want it, and what you want people to say about you, everything you do actually influences and works its way back into your story. This includes your family. I tell my children this, too. When you're out there, you're not just representing yourself; you're representing your family. My children are representing me as their father who's working and the things that I'm trying to do for their benefit. Their good behavior and character make it better for me. That's the story that gets out. "Well, not only is Orlando a good guy, but he's raised two other good guys!" That helps me, which helps them. All those things kind of intersect and interplay.

And, I love traveling with my sons.

As you work toward senior leadership, including the C-suite, you become a representative of your company brand. Your brand becomes a part of the company brand. It's not just your technical competence that they're hiring; they're also buying your brand. They're asking themselves whether your brand, connected to their brand, will enhance the total brand. This is why the invitations become more intimate as you go up the chain. It goes from just having a drink after dinner to having dinner, to having dinner with you and your spouse (and your boss and his or her spouse), to "Why don't you come to our summer home? Why don't we travel and go hang out for the weekend?" That continuum of time together is also a function of the level on which you want to play, and the integration of your brand and the other person's brand.

For young people, what I think is important to do is to "reverse mentor" your bosses. What I mean by reverse mentoring is sharing knowledge that you have with those above you that they don't have that same context. I did some reverse mentoring around being African American. I put the article in my boss's inbox on managing a person of color, and he read it and made some decisions about creating mentorship opportunities for me based on that article.

Oftentimes, people of older generations are looking for help. I'm 52, so I'm old enough to be probably more like the Boomers and that generation, but I'm young enough to be able to try to connect with young people. For me, understanding young people is important, and some of the best working relationships I've had have been with young people who were willing to help me out. One of my mentees, Sophia, played that role for me. While I was her boss, she would coach me on things that were more in tune with her age group. That was helpful, and I think there are opportunities for young people to build and create those relationships based on their expertise.

While those of us who are older would like to understand the culture of young people today, we often don't know how. Studies show that by 2025, millennials will make up around 40 percent of the workforce. I think it's an opportunity to create connections, relationships, and intimacy in a sponsorship role which has value moving forward. I would argue that I've definitely taken on a sponsorship kind of posture with Sophia. And she is one of those people who I would hire and rehire over the course of my career.

It's all about connection

Networking has been framed as a numbers game–seeing how many business cards you can collect while attending an event. For too many people, networking is about the number of people you meet, or it's about asking people to do things for you, as opposed to making a connection where you both benefit.

After all, the true goal of a networking event is to create a connection with other people at an event–preferably people who understand that as well. It's about starting up and creating the spark of a new relationship. Once you create that connection, then the opportunities flow from there. Gathering 800 business cards at an event doesn't get you anywhere, and the truth is that most people just throw those cards away. Creating a connection, rather than just collecting a card, is making the event purposeful.

Connecting works because when we connect, we care about the other person. And when we care about the other person, we become invested in their success as well as our own. We don't just see them as John Doe, director of purchasing. We see them as John Doe, father of three, golfer, military veteran, community leader, and recreational runner. When we see people for who they are, where they fit in their community and the work they do, we relate to the things we have in common. It's just as I discovered as class president–when we focus on how we're alike, what we have in common, and what common goals we share, then we can work towards a greater good that benefits us all.

When I understand who others are, what's important to them, and where they spend their time and interests, then I can see where their networks lie, and I can improve both my network and theirs. The resources we share expand as do the opportunities. That's what networking truly is, expanding everyone's resources and opportunities. Together we can become greater than any one of us can by ourselves.

You may be a great networker or a poor one. You may have a lot of skills to develop and practice before your networking skills become a part of you. And, that's what they have to be, to be truly successful.

> You have to naturally express interest in others and look for ways you can help them before you even think about how they can help you.

Networking is definitely a social skill, but it's more than that. It's a character trait. It's something the C-suite looks for – an ability to work with others, to get along, to have a relationship with a great variety of people in a cordial, friendly, professionally intimate way.

If you work on any skill on a daily basis, this is the one it should be. You should be learning how to connect, and to connect with people like you, people not like you, and people who don't have anything in common with you at first glance. If you're in a situation where you can't do that, then you need to put yourself in a situation where you can.

Visit a part of the city you've never been to before. Go to a different city. Take a vacation in Canada, or another country. Go on a cruise. Join a meet-up group or take a class. Put yourself in situations where you'll meet people who aren't like you. Then practice your connecting and networking skills. If you bomb, you can always go back. Try again. Keep trying. When it becomes comfortable, stretch yourself. Push yourself. Try another arena where you're not comfortable and keep doing that. Ultimately your efforts will pay off.

Learning how to hear what is not being said

When you are networking you will meet people who may say one thing but have ulterior motives or intentions. This is where the ability to read someone's body language becomes an important skill. I told the story before about going to the Lebanese restaurant in Dubai with friends and not speaking the language but having so much fun I returned the next night by myself. How was I able to understand them so well while not speaking their language?

Having spent time in so many countries where English was not the primary language, I developed the ability to communicate beyond words–reading hand motions, body language, facial expressions and sensing the energy from others. This skill has served me here in the States where there are times when I talk with people and they say one thing, but their body language shows me they are basically saying something very different. So, if you don't have time to get the out-of-country education I had the good fortune of getting, consider picking up a book or two on body language.

Taking networking to the next level

Once you have developed the skill of networking, you will want to invest in the next level of connecting which is developing a network of mentors, and then sponsors. In the next chapter we'll examine the differences between these two and how to connect with people who can become your mentor or sponsor most effectively.

More than any other, the seventh principle of developing and nurturing your career community is critical to enabling your career success. This process takes time and effort, but I encourage you to embrace it. This is an opportunity to develop powerful, insightful relationships with people that will invest in you and you in them. Your career community will help enhance your career, but more importantly, it will make you a better person. Enjoy the journey.

"In order to be irreplaceable, one must always be different."

—Coco Chanel

CHAPTER 8
The Power of Being Different

We come to the eighth and final principle: understanding how being different from your colleagues in the workplace gives you an edge. For years many have felt that being different was a hurdle or obstacle that needs to be managed. But I would argue that being different can actually be an advantage, and when executed deftly, can be an accelerator in your career.

As I have said before, I'm a tall, 230 lb., African American male, so people have to quickly ascertain who and/or what I am. Some have made incorrect assumptions over the years, but I've become very good at taking a person from where they might think I am to how I want them to see me—a cool father, an author or an executive.

This is a message to those of you who have spent a considerable amount of time *fitting* in to help you be ok with *fitting* out and leveraging that to your advantage. Of course, shifting this perspective and then taking action doesn't mean there won't be any pain involved, but, trust me, it will be worth it.

As an executive, there is power in having a self-awareness in your difference and then building your teams accordingly. I have a background in organizational development, business strategy, and communications. I make sure to have the very best talent in other skills, such as finance, on my team. We all have our points of difference, and rather than look at it as a hurdle, there is strength in looking at it as a point of genius.

Collective intelligence

People often ask me what has been one of my keys to success. How have I been able to continue to take on new opportunities in different industries and even live abroad? Again, they may ask me, "How DID you get that job?" I share with them that one of my approaches has been to tap into the collective intelligence around me. Scott Page, author of the book *The Difference*, shares the premise that diverse teams deliver exceptional results. Meaning, if you create an environment that allows you tap into the collective intelligence of a diverse team, you will outperform other, homogeneous teams. Throughout the years I have worked to form groups that are diverse in the broadest sense possible. Using this strategy,

I have indeed been able to out-perform and out-deliver others.

For example, I was considered an unorthodox choice when I was selected to be the president of Holland America Line. So there have been some who asked: How do you take a person who has never been on a cruise ship and ask him to lead that second longest-running cruise line in the world, invigorate the brand, engage the crew to new levels, and improve the profit trajectory of the business? My job wasn't to "out cruise line" others with 10-50 years of experience in the industry. My goal was to lead, which also included helping employees take the good ideas they may have had for years that for, whatever reason, had yet to be implemented, and let them unleash them. As a result, a lot of great new things happened. A few of our accomplishments included:

- From the music space, we revolutionized the onboard experience for our guests, designing the best music venues at sea, which included BB King's Blues Club, Lincoln Center Stage, Rolling Stone Rock Room, and Billboard Onboard.
- Enhanced our culinary offerings with Tamarind, Nami Sushi, Rudi's Sel de Mer, added world-renowned wine critic, James Suckling, to the team, and expanded our Culinary Council to include celebrated chef, Ethan Stowell, Sushi Chef, Andy Matsuda, "Top Chef" winner, Kristen Kish, and James Beard Award-winner, Edouardo Jordan.

- Unique wine partnerships with Chateau St. Michelle, a customized wine experience we called Blend.
- We announced a new partnership with BBC earth, AFAR, America's Test Kitchen, and O, the Oprah Winfrey magazine.
- And, as a result of our strong relationship with the magazine, we were honored to have Oprah Winfrey serve as the godmother of our latest ship, Nieuw Statendam.

There is collective intelligence in a diverse team. However, if you don't tap into this diverse intelligence, you could end up with a team that underperforms. While a company's ambition is to continuously grow, I would argue that each company needs to figure out how to create an environment that pulls the rich value out of diverse teams.

Here, people need to feel comfortable sharing and innovating. The way I do this is more about setting up an environment where people are encouraged to participate. The cruise line environment takes their management cues from the navy, and there is significant hierarchy within the industry. I had been in the business at Holland America Line for just two weeks when one of my leaders in fleet operations came to see me to discuss an issue. When he finished sharing the issue with me, he paused, and waited for me to make a decision. I asked him, "How long he have you been here?" And he answered, "22 years," to which I replied, "I've been here two weeks, which one of us is in the best position to make this decision?" Clearly it was him. While technically I was the boss, it would have been poor leadership for me to make the decision.

As a leader, I've always been comfortable knowing what I know, but equally as comfortable knowing what I don't know, and allowing those with the appropriate expertise to lead in their areas of knowledge.

As I mentioned, in the beginning there were people who would avoid getting into the elevator with me or even just avoid eye contact because they didn't know me. I would say in meetings, "Hey, I don't bite. I invite you to connect with me." It didn't happen overnight, but with regular encouragement and reinforcing a positive response to anyone in the company who did connect, by the time I left the company five and a half years later, employees didn't hesitate to say hello in the elevator, hallway or lunchroom, or send me an email to share their thoughts.

Building a powerful culture: Responding versus reacting

Several years ago, I was scheduled to meet with a couple of consultants at my office in New York City, and I waited in the conference room for them to arrive. When they showed up, I heard my assistant greet them and say, "Orlando's waiting for you in the first conference room on the left." I heard them approach the conference room where I waited, but when they came through the door, they looked at me and said, "Oh–sorry, sir. Wrong room," and they spun on their heels, to then proceed down to the *second* conference room on the left. There was nobody in the room, so they sat down to wait for "Orlando."

Why did that happen? Well, it was clear it was because they didn't consider that I could be the person they were there to see.

Now, in that moment I had a decision to make. I could ignore it, I could get offended or defensive, or I could turn it into an opportunity to create some power. I found very early on that while sometimes there are words to gently move someone from their pre-conceived notions and take them to where I need them to be, it doesn't always work. For example, I could have offered cues like: "You're coming up to 44 to see me," when the 44th floor is the executive floor. But there is only so much one can do to help move people from seeing things in the context of their biases. And after the fact, it felt too egregious to just ignore, but reacting with anger wouldn't have been productive either.

When people react, they are emotional and can often get out of control. On the other hand, when they *respond,* they figure out a way to take action to move the situation in the direction of the desired outcome. So, in the case of these two gentlemen, I responded by calling the friend of mine who sent them to explain to him what had happened. While I did not react in front of them, I was still upset, and I explained my frustration. As a result of my response and our further conversations, this company asked me to teach a small diversity workshop to their employees–including these two men. In fact, I've returned there several times to hold similar sessions for their teams.

Another time, I was in a boardroom with several other colleagues for a meeting that was about to begin. A vendor was there to pitch his business to the leadership team, including our CFO. As one of our female associates walked by him, the vendor said to her, "Hey honey, can you please get me some coffee with cream?" The woman left the room and returned with coffee with cream for him, and then she sat down at the head of the table to start the meeting. She was the CFO. The look on the vendor's face was priceless, as in that moment he realized that she had the power to tank this whole deal because of his treatment of her just moments earlier. The entire decision came through her. She also had a decision to make: ignore it, get angry, or turn it into an opportunity to create some power. She chose the latter, and even though he apologized for his mistake, she didn't let him off the hook and she made him really work to pitch for their business. She took back the power.

These examples and countless others have taught me:

> Your response is a choice you have, with the possibility for you to create a much more positive outcome.

In fact, this realization goes back to that moment I was hit by that snowball at the age of 19. I realized from my father's advice that I had choices, and the better choice was to challenge myself to look at the "bigger picture" as to what was going on. It doesn't mean you have to sell out or ignore how you feel. Rather, it means winning the war, achieving your goal, being successful, so you will eventually be in a position to change things.

Life isn't always fair

I've spent the first part of this book providing things that you can do to enable yourselves to accelerate your career. The reality of the world we live in is that it can be difficult, and it isn't always fair, but it is changing. With a pandemic and worldwide economic collapse worse than anything we've seen in more than 100 years, plus the killing of George Floyd and protests for racial justice in cities around the world, it's safe to say that most of us have all been pushed in ways we never expected.

And a broad array of Americans–black, brown and white–are finally ready to have difficult conversations and drive change.

We've had reason before to hope the tide might be shifting. In 2008, we elected our first black President of the United States, and many thought we were finally coming together as a country; that an era of hope and healing was upon us. In 2018, the movie *Black Panther*, with its embrace of Black actors and African traditions, had become the ninth highest grossing movie of all time. These seemed to be good indicators that we, as a country, might be moving in the right direction to address racial perceptions and social injustice.

But this would not appear to fully be the case. While some positive progress has been made, so much is still the same.

In 2016, shortly after Philando Castile was pulled over and fatally shot by the police, I found myself teaching my own son to drive, and what to do if–and when–he is pulled over. For his first lesson, he sat in the driver's seat and I coached him to take out his wallet before the officer arrives at the window, place his driver's license on the dashboard, keep his hands on the wheel at 10 and 2, and be very respectful.

And as I role-played the officer, I realized that my father had taught me this same lesson more than 30 years ago when I was 17. Nothing at all had changed. The fear my father had for me, I now had for my son. So much progress, but so much is still the same.

But there is hope.

In this period of such unrest and uncertainty, I've had more open dialog about race with my fellow board directors and executive colleagues than I have in the last several years. I'm encouraged by these discussions and what it might mean for change in this country.

There is a theory in behavioral psychology called an "extinction burst," when one sees a sudden increase in a behavior's intensity and frequency, followed by its decline and ultimate extinction when the subject refuses to reinforce it.

I believe this may be what we're seeing today–an extinction burst may be underway. A national momentum has been building against hate and bigotry from people of all races, and as unsettling as some of what we've seen can be, I'm encouraged that across the country we are seeing a real shift toward the eradication of extreme racism and social injustice. And with that shift, a platform for everyone of all different backgrounds to pursue and excel in their career ambitions, now more than ever.

Last thoughts

Thank you for being ambitious and wanting something more from your career. It has been an honor to share these eight principles that I have learned, seen, and used in my time working in corporate America.

My ambition in writing this book was simply to be helpful. I've been blessed with great parents who helped me believe I could be or do anything. I developed a strong network of friends and advisors who challenged and counseled me as I made major decisions throughout the course of my career. I've been given some extremely challenging opportunities that made me stretch and truly changed the trajectory of my career. I've had the opportunity to do things both personally and professionally that I never truly expected and have been able to achieve things beyond my wildest visions. But I'm not quite done yet. I believe I have a few more things to learn and achieve in the remaining part of my career.

My hope is that by sharing these principles I've learned, and my personal stories of both challenge and triumph, you will be able to accelerate your own career trajectory. I want you to take these principles and try them.

Challenge yourself. Envision what you want your future to look like and work on your foundational soft skills. Earn a reputation as someone who delivers results and think big, start small, and move fast. Be a culture builder and storyteller in your organization and pay close attention to building your personal brand. Invest in developing your career community and embrace the power of being different.

Leverage the things that we've covered, and it will allow you the opportunity to soar toward career success.

My wish for you: all the success that you strive for in work, and in life.

"Oh, to be young again."
–Unknown

BONUS CHAPTER

Young People–Your Education and Experience is All You Really Own

So, why am I offering advice to young people? While I'm definitely not one, I'm working with them more and more and learning from them, and while I believe we need to learn and evolve, some of our "old school ways" still have some merit.

Amass experience first

When I came out of college, I'd already had nine internships with five different companies. That was unique. Thanks to the corporate internship program I was in throughout high school, I've been working in corporate America since I was 14. I'm a bit unusual from that perspective. That early start in the workforce is why I think my career accelerated as fast as it did. I amassed a great deal of experience before I graduated from college, and since I've been out of college working full-time, I've worked for a number of different companies: Andersen Consulting, Ameritech, Delta Consulting, Motorola, Coca-Cola, Marsh & McLennan, Mercer, and most recently, Holland America Line.

Speaking from my personal experience, I recommend you build up your toolkit of experiences and knowledge. You want a breadth of experiences for yourself. Not only will you enjoy your life more and create wisdom and insights into people better than through any other endeavor, you'll build a collection of knowledge, experiences, and achievements that will add value to your opinions, advice, and words.

For instance, for someone who wants to speak about working internationally, you'll want to do your research and internalize what you learn. Of course, if you've traveled internationally, your words may have more value. If you've lived and worked internationally, then your insights will have even more value. And if you've lived abroad for an extended period of time in multiple countries like I have, then you can count yourself as an expert and may be sought for your thoughts on the subject.

What is it you're interested in and most passionate about, and how can you build up a set of experiences and education and knowledge about those subjects? Can you grow a track record of impact and success in those areas? As you build that out, your toolkit, your words, and your experience will have incremental value. The better the value, the more likely you'll be to figure out how to trade that value for whatever it is you want, financially or otherwise. That's sort of how I think about it. Your career journey is about collecting that experience, collecting that education, and then hopefully delivering impact and trading that with organizations or corporations that will pay you for your experience.

Military boot camp lasts 13 weeks. And it's not just 13 long weeks of hard work, every phase is structured and coordinated for a specific purpose and end. Recruits must be trained, acclimated, and conditioned before they can start their careers as military men and women. If they aren't prepared, they will fail. Many trades and professions, including plumbers, electricians, carpenters, printers, seafarers, and other hands-on occupations also require new members to apprentice before they become recognized professionals. It's a way to make sure newcomers to a trade have the hands-on experience to do the job.

While many of us think that book learning is all we need to succeed, the truth is that experience is far more valuable. Experience is more valuable because when we have experience coupled with the actual skill itself, we also gain some degree of expertise in the soft skills: communication, foresight, hindsight, timing, and all the emotional, intellectual, and non-specific skills that come from experience.

For instance, someone who has worked with children as a camp counselor, coach, or teacher is more likely to understand children once they have children of their own. Conversely, if you have children and interact with them frequently, you are more likely to be able to understand and work with children in a different setting. It's the people skills—the soft skills—which you develop as you go that make you better.

Coaches, particularly high school coaches, get better over time, not because they get better at athletic skills, but because they get better at people skills. They get better at motivating teenagers and understanding how to discipline and inspire their teams, coaches, and managers. They also learn how to deal with parents and hone the soft skills of leadership, which makes them better leaders and coaches. College, boot camp, apprenticeships, internships, and just the plain old school of hard knocks can teach us these practical skills. It takes practice and hands-on work over time to gain the experience we need, coupled with education, to become truly gifted.

Ideally, universities and colleges condition, train, and acclimate students to their chosen careers. It's up to the student to find or seek out the opportunity to experience what they've learned. Unfortunately, most of what is available in college requires students to be proactive and seek out the opportunity, which is something they often have no experience doing. No one is going to force you to attend classes, join study groups and clubs, or be active. It's up to you, the student, to make the most of the educational opportunities and you can only do that if you know which college offers the most of what you're looking for before you apply.

Just as each military service, trade, or profession has its own reputation, challenges, brand, and personality, so does each college. Some are better than others at nudging students and helping them get the experience they need to succeed. It's up to you to research and find out whether a college will help you get where you want to go.

The time you spend in college should get you more than a degree. It will get you the experience that often adds up to more than the education. Experience is what you get from your internships, network, friends, mentors, emotional and career support, and overall, your brand. It only makes sense to take time and choose your college wisely.

Choosing the traditional college experience

If you choose the traditional college route–four years at a college or university–do your due diligence. Research the schools you are interested in attending before committing and applying.

It's possible to take a few classes, have the idea and talent you need to succeed, and never darken the door of a college. There are pros and cons to attending college, including a community college. You will learn and experience things in college that you won't have a chance to experience in the world. You'll meet people from different economic and social backgrounds that you may not have immediate access to outside of college. Plus, enrollment in a college or university is almost always a requirement for any internship in any field, and internships are the gateway to being hired immediately, right out of college. By the time you've completed one or two internships with a company, they know whether they like you and vice versa.

There are other acceptable options as well, including community college, technical college, online classes, and certificate programs. Keep in mind that college is just one part of your toolbox. Work and travel experience, social skills, networking, and other abilities create the overall set of experiences you want.

College is an important, yet expensive proposition. My challenge to you is to attend as much and as good of a college as you can afford.

When you are ready to select a college, base your choice on as many of these criteria as possible:

- **REPUTATION.** Every college has a reputation, a brand. What's it known for? What's it's specialty?

Here's a trick that I learned that you could also try when you're looking at schools--buy a shirt or a hat from the campus store and wear it when you get back home, then pay attention to the reactions you get from people. You will have similar reactions for the rest of your life if you choose to attend that school.

Why is a school's reputation so important? Reputation is the currency of the world. If you're not sure of a school's reputation or ranking, check out "Forbes Top American University's" list to see where your school ranks. Some schools rank higher for certain specialties. If you want to make a career in the military, attending any one of the military academies is a tremendous goal and will serve you better than merely enrolling and finishing basic training in the same service. Even getting admitted to a military school is an honor, and graduating, especially if you rank high in your class, is a bonus.

That said, Bill Gates, Steve Jobs, and many other billionaires and well-known and respected men and women never graduated from college. It's important to note that Gates was admitted to Harvard, where he met Steve Ballmer, who would later take over Gates' role as CEO of Microsoft from January 2000 to February 2014.

One of the many benefits of college is the opportunity to meet people from other parts of the country, financial strata, and background that you might not meet otherwise. College classes can also be the catalyst for a career or an idea that spawns a career. At a minimum, it's the place to begin to build your career network.

Steve Jobs briefly attended Reed College, the only private undergraduate college in the United States with a primarily student-run nuclear reactor supporting its science programs. Reed College is also known for its unusually high proportion of graduates, and many of its graduates go on to earn PhDs and other postgraduate degrees. Although Steve Jobs is not among their numbered grads, he obviously made his mark. What changed the world, Jobs told a graduating class at Stanford, was that he took a calligraphy class at Reed. From that calligraphy class came the concept of fonts for the Mac, a feature most computer users now take for granted. If he hadn't taken that calligraphy class, chances are technology and graphics wouldn't be where they are today.

It's a fact of life--people, companies, corporations, and politicians decide with whom to collaborate, do business, or endorse. A school's name and reputation is worth whatever you have to spend to attend. This holds true for seminars, conferences, and any training you receive. If all people have is your education by which to judge you, they will do just that. You're not just investing in your education; you're investing in your reputation. The Times' Higher-Education World University Rankings site has the highest, best reputation for ranking schools, and is taken more seriously than other ratings since those ratings are entirely the result of a poll of scholars, not students.

- **SOCIAL STRUCTURE.** The people you get to know and bond with during your college years are the people you are most likely to keep in touch with throughout your career. What a lot of people don't realize is that you meet the most people you'll know in college during your freshman year. You'll still meet people every semester, but the opportunities to meet new people will become more and more limited as you progress and immerse yourselves in your programs, internships, and opportunities in your career field. The same is true for the other students as well. How many opportunities, clubs, meetings, and study groups are there for students in your field? Are there extracurricular activities? Competitions? Teams? Clubs? Meetups? Will you be able to network at school, and on a national or regional level with other students?

- **CULTURE.** Every college has a personality. If you want to feel like a part of the college experience, your personality has to feel comfortable with that of the school itself. You've got to be able to find one or more clubs, niches, and groups where you feel like you belong. If you're a woman or a person of color, are you looking at colleges where diversity is promoted? Determining a college's culture or personality takes some trial and error, but it can be done. Spend time on campus. Take a tour. Talk to students. Attend orientation at the college. Read any news stories you can find about the college. Speak with some of your potential future professors. Do more than visit the university's website, written by marketing professionals. It's designed to show the college in the best possible light. Do your research to get a sense of the school's culture and vibe.
- **FINANCIAL AID.** Does the school offer financial aid? Are you eligible? Are there work-study programs as well as grants, loans, and other options for you?
- **GRADUATION RATE.** What is the graduation rate? How many students drop out each semester and why? What are your chances, given testing and test scores, that you'll finish school?
- **NUMBER OF ADVISORS.** Are student advisors assigned to every student? How much time can you expect to spend

with them? Is there a counseling center you can go to if you're feeling stressed, worried, pressured, or uncertain?

• **PLACEMENT RECORD.** Does the college you're considering have a job placement program? Do they help students get internships and interviews? Do they have staff who help students learn to prepare and study for interviews or research potential companies? Do they help graduating students enter the work force or do they just stand in the doorway and wave goodbye? Check their website to see what placement services they offer. A good placement office will help students find jobs and internships while they are in school, as well as after graduation. Contact some recent alumni of the school and ask them about their experience with job placement.

• **ALUMNI.** Who are the alumni of the school that you are considering? These will be the people in your network if you end up attending this school. What is their relationship with the school? Is it positive? Are they active in supporting and being a part of the school or have they just moved on and lost touch? Do they have good feelings and memories of the school? Check with LinkedIn and Facebook to find the names of alumni of different schools. Go to your local library or look online to find and read the alumni magazines and publications from each school you are considering. Do they feature alumni prominently in the magazines? Many schools see alumni only as potential fundraising targets while others support and share the success of their former grads like proud parents. The publications they print will tell you what you want to know.

• **POLITICAL AND BUSINESS ALLIANCES.** Your profession matters. If you plan to go into politics, law, or a field where you'll be dealing with the reputation or brand you've established for yourself throughout college, it's important to understand who the local alliances, state representatives and officials are. Who are they? What is their reputation? Are they ethical? Moral? Fair? How involved are they with the college? Are they on a Board of Directors? Do they contribute in any advisory capacities?

• **ACCESS TO PROFESSORS.** How much actual access will you have to your professors? This can be important, especially if you do well and want a recommendation later for an internship or interview. If you go on college tours, sit in on some classes and talk to students in those classes. If you're not doing college tours, find forums or websites online where students rank their professors.

Other approaches to education

Pursuing a four-year degree at a college or university is no longer your only option for getting an education. However, the caveats remain the same: If you choose to pursue other learning options, take time to evaluate and select the best program for you and your goals. Ultimately, you want to make decisions based on whether or not you will gain the experience and education needed to get you where you want to go. Many times, you can get what you want without a college degree. There are professions such as law, medicine, and engineering that require a degree for licensing and to practice. But, if you want to be an entrepreneur, you have many more options for getting an education that will serve you well.

Options for getting a great education outside of a four-year program include:

- **COMMUNITY COLLEGE.** Community colleges offer specialized, hands-on classes where you get to actually practice the skills you're learning. In the past, community colleges offered mostly trade classes – welding, carpentry, electrical, and other professions. In addition to those, now they offer photography, graphic design, business administration, technology, and almost all the career options that a four-year program offers. Many two-year colleges also offer less expensive classes that will transfer to a four-year college if you choose to go that route.
- **APPRENTICESHIPS.** Apprenticeships have traditionally been offered primarily in the trades, including the stock market, photography, welding, carpentry, plumbing and so forth. Motivated students have found that by approaching and pitching a company for whom they know they want to work, whether it's a local nursery or accounting firm, they can land an apprenticeship. Apprenticeships generally involve an offer to work for a company or individual for free or a nominal wage for a period of time (usually three to six months) in exchange for training in that field. As an apprentice, you skip the administrative tasks like filing and mail delivery and get actual hands-on training for the position by the experts currently

doing the job. It's often unpaid, but consider it getting a free education in exchange for some sweat equity.

Also, you can often find a small business that is not quite able to hire someone but needs the extra help to expand. They are much more likely to take on an apprentice, especially if they believe or see you have potential to be an asset.

If you're enrolled in college, a similar experience is called an "internship." Depending on the internship, you may be doing entry-level tasks no one else wants to do while watching from afar as others do the actual work, or you may be given the opportunity to do some real work and get involved in actual projects. It depends on the internship.

Convincing a corporation or organization to bring you on board for an apprenticeship takes great sales skills. Most companies understand the nature of internships. Not many are willing to risk an apprenticeship with someone not enrolled in college classes. If you're older, with work experience and a career history, you may stand a better chance of an apprenticeship because you have existing job skills that you can bring to the table. Whether you get an apprenticeship or not, the practice of pitching several companies will hone your sales abilities.

- **INTERNSHIPS.** An internship, unlike an apprenticeship, allows for more exploration, testing, and experimenting with a position to see if you like it or not. Apprenticeships are usually dedicated positions for those who have decided they want to be a mechanic, a welder or another specific profession or trade.

When you start you know you're there to receive instruction from a craftsman or expert in that trade. Internships tend to be more of a buffet, with a chance to sample several projects and the company itself. Internships also provide an opportunity to show a company what you're capable of, often leading to job offers after you graduate.

Internships can be paid or unpaid. If the internship is unpaid, it's usually subject to more stringent labor guidelines. Federal law mandates that unpaid interns must not benefit the company economically or be used to displace the work done by paid employees. Each state has its own regulations regarding interns. Almost all states require interns to receive college credit for their work.

For me personally, internships were the single biggest accelerator of my career. Being able to start early and begin to understand the technical aspects of how corporations worked allowed me to figure out what I wanted to do and what I did not want to do.

Online free education. Free, online classes are a great way to get an education, even if you don't get certification or any official evidence of completing a course successfully. Many universities and colleges are rushing to offer these classes, and more are offered every year.

Education of all forms is an incredible career prepping experience, or it can be. It's where you first start learning how to make connections, network, and spot fellow classmates who may be great members of your career community one day.

Young people entering the workforce

While young people have time on their side, they often don't have the experience they need to hit the ground running. At a minimum, this will involve learning and developing the skills more seasoned professionals have had to learn, but the following are some things I learned along the way that I hope will help you in your journey:

- **DO WHAT YOU LOVE.** Why work for 20, 30 or 40 years doing something you hate or aren't passionate about? Yes, you may end up taking a job for a while where you wear your name on your shirt (which can be a very good thing), just to pay the bills. But if this isn't your ambition, learn from it and use your situation to figure out what you truly love.
- **DEVELOP A UNIQUE SKILL SET.** Don't just be someone doing a job anyone with a warm body and some direction can do. Develop skills to take with you wherever you go. It doesn't matter if it's plumbing, welding, carpentry, or cuisine, or a law, medical, professional, or mechanical skill. You should have skills that set you apart if you want a career. If you don't have them, then develop them – college, internship, apprenticeship, or practice.
- **NETWORK, NETWORK, NETWORK.** This doesn't just mean handing out business cards at conferences. It means developing relationships with people in your industry, or your desired industry.
- **USE YOUR SOCIAL NETWORKS** (TikTok, SnapChat,

Facebook, LinkedIn, Twitter, Instagram, Reddit, etc.) to stay connected, engaged, and visible.

• **DRESS FOR SUCCESS.** Yes, there are companies that embrace a casual appearance, but dressing up still speaks loudly and commands the respect you'll need to get the dream job you're wanting. Even the way you approach casual dress can make a statement. Casual doesn't mean sloppy. I think a smart casual style can speak louder than a suit when executed properly. It comes down to the message you want to send.

• **NEVER STOP LEARNING.** Even after graduation you can still take classes, get certificates, and pursue the "fun" stuff you never took in college. Steve Jobs dropped out of college, but he took a class in calligraphy and the rest (fonts for Mac) is history. You never know where a class will take you and don't even try to figure it out. Just follow your curiosity. Do what you love, learn what you love, and keep learning in all areas that interest you. You'll use it later in life, I promise.

• **BE FINANCIALLY RESPONSIBLE AND PAY YOUR BILLS.** Employers check credit reports and a bad report can shut you out of a great job. It really can.

• **BE FISCALLY SAVVY.** Many young people have already learned to avoid credit cards and debt acquired by buying houses and cars. If you haven't, start becoming more financially literate. Read "Young Money" by Todd Romer, or take some classes to learn how to save, invest, and make smart money decisions. Owning your financial health gives you more control over your career health.

Start early: take care of yourself

You're just starting out, so I can take this moment to urge you not to make the same mistakes I made. First, with regard to your health, an obvious one–pay attention. All parents say, "Pay attention now–you'll be my age someday, and you'll wish you had." I'm tooting the same horn, but the horn has always been right. There's no new magic there, it's just true. You feel indestructible, unbeatable, as a young person, but even superstar athletes pay attention to their bodies in very significant ways. That's true for us.

Do what you can to keep your brain sharp. If you're going to play the corporate game, your brain is your best muscle. Are you building and training and developing that muscle? Have you thought about that? Training your brain wasn't even a concept when I was coming up. But, now, brain games are available everywhere that challenge and are meant to help strengthen your brain and mental reflexes.

The next best tip I can give you is to manage your finances in a way that gives you career control. Here's what I mean. The way the game was played back in my day, a person would be brought into corporate with the expectation that they would want to take the vacations, buy a house and a car, have two kids, send them to college, etc. Those financial expectations create indebtedness to a company that forced the person to become somewhat trapped into staying with the company even if they wanted to leave.

Maintaining financial flexibility will empower you to make stronger decisions relative to your career. You should be able to make a choice about a job or opportunity without having to worry about your short-term finances.

Live within your means, or below your means. Or, again–playing multiple chess boards here–manage your finances in a way that does not indebt you to your job. You don't want to be in a position where you can't make a decision, you can't make a move on any other chess board, and you can't walk away. I'm a student of Robert Kiyosaki–*Rich Dad, Poor Dad.* He talks about taking your money and positioning it and investing it in a way so that your money works for you and you're not just working for money. Right, wrong, or indifferent, in a corporate setting, you are working for money. Hopefully you're successful, and your ability to create more money increases over time., but you are working for a salary, which means you are spending your time making wealth for someone else. If you're able to take portions of that salary and position it so that it helps pay you then you have added flexibility. That can be writing a book, building a website, creating an app, or building a brand that enables you to do speaking engagements for which you can charge ten or twenty thousand dollars–in *addition* to what you do in a corporate setting. Having that flexibility, or building towards that flexibility, will allow you to be more in control of the decisions that you're making relative to your career.

And the best part? In all my time as an HR executive, I saw

that the best-performing employees were those with the best personal, financial, and career health. Do you have the skills and knowledge that are important to be effective in your job? If so, that's the focus of most companies, but are you physically healthy? Are your brain and body in a good position so that you can actually show up to work and deliver? More people are beginning to think about that.

Also, is your financial situation healthy? If you're in debt, or you're going to lose your house or your car, or you're worried about your children or your retirement, you can't show up as your best self. That's true at the corporate level, but that's definitely true at the individual level. Those three things all feed on each other. If your finances aren't well, then you're stressed, which hurts your physical health, which then hurts your ability to perform, and thus your career health. All those health buckets play on one another. You want to think about all three in order to be a sustainable, vibrant, executive leader. Start thinking about all of these things now. You'll have the benefit of starting earlier than most of us, which can be a career accelerator for you.

ACKNOWLEDGMENTS

I have a lot of people to thank who have influenced this book. First and foremost, I'm thankful to my family, who continually support and inspire me to challenge myself. Finishing this book was their latest challenge. Thank you.

Obie, Grace, Samantha, Orlando II, and **Jackson.**

Additionally, I want to thank my team of close colleagues. They are really more than colleagues, they are my friends, and they helped me make this book happen with their insight, counsel, and even energized debate. I appreciate their help.

Kim Fuqua (my editor), **Doug Parks, Billy Dexter,** and **Michelle Sutter.**

There are numerous leaders and bosses (both good and bad), who I need to thank as well. I have learned from each of them and they have inspired much of the learning reflected in this book. There are too many to name, but I want to acknowledge them all.

Made in USA - North Chelmsford, MA
1179479_9781952779053
10.13.2020 0815